TEAMMATES FOR LIFE

MARTY GALLAGHER

Angier Publishing

DEDICATION

I have been blessed to be surrounded by wonderful people my entire life. People I could always rely upon for friendship, advice, laughter and strength. My siblings – Maggie, Dan, Joe, Tim, Katie, Ed and Jerry – are seven of the greatest people I will ever meet. They have been supportive of everything that I have ever attempted … and they have inspired me by the way they live their lives.

But I would like to dedicate this book to my dad, Don, and my wife, Emily.

I learned to love sports by watching my dad and seeing how passionate he was about following his favorite teams. Whether it was the local high school team, the Iowa Hawkeyes, Chicago Cubs, Chicago Bears … or even a seventh-grade team if he had a child playing, Dad would always react enthusiastically to any successes. And if things didn't go well, he wouldn't hold back much then, either. His heart was on his sleeve for everyone to see and hear. Referees might have found him to be a bit too "spirited" at times through the years, but that's probably a story for another day. Nobody enjoys watching sports more than my dad.

My dad has also always been a person to get things done. My parents raised eight children, attended our games and events, instilled a strong work ethic, supported us every step of the way ... and still had time to spend with each other and maintain their sanity. Dad also always had a "cause" that he was working toward, whether it was keeping the local golf course afloat or supporting the local booster club. Somehow, he seemed to always be working toward a goal and I don't think I ever saw him fall short.

Someone full of wisdom once pointed out that adversity reveals a person's true character. I think there's a lot of truth to that. From the time my mother was diagnosed with breast cancer in the spring of 2005 until she passed away in January of 2009, my dad was an absolute rock. His love for her was evident when I was growing up, but during those years she was sick, he did *everything* he could do for her. My dad has always been outgoing and enjoys conversation ... he's never met a stranger. But when Mom was sick, Dad let his actions do the talking. He provided her with the support she needed and the dignity she deserved. In the end, they were holding hands when she drew her last breath.

For a thousand reasons, my dad is my hero.

My wife Emily is the most beautiful person I will ever know. She is gorgeous, intelligent, funny and has a magnificent smile, but she also has the kindest heart I have ever witnessed. I am continually amazed at how she sees the best in people and her empathy has no limits. You cannot spend any time with her without becoming a better person. Our five children are incredibly lucky to have such a selfless role model.

When I decided to write this book, Emily knew that it would mean I would need to spend several hours of "family time" in my office – away from her and the kids – in order to complete this project. She couldn't have been more supportive of me taking the time necessary to write … and she also served as my main advisor.

I spent the first couple of decades of my life growing up, then it took a little more time to figure out what I wanted to do for a living. But there was something missing. Then, I met Emily and ever since that day, I've been happy.

For a thousand reasons, Emily is my best friend and my inspiration.

Thank you, Dad and Emily, for all you do … and for the examples you've both set for our family. You are the best. I love you.

Contents

INTRODUCTION

The following is a true story that I've told bits and pieces of several times in the past year or two. Frequently, the response is something like, "That would make a good book … someone should write about that."

I agree. I think it's a great story.

As a basketball fan who grew up in Iowa in the 1980s, this is a subject that is close to my heart. But ultimately, this is *not* a basketball story.

This is an uplifting story about lasting friendships, and what we are willing to do for those we love.

Fighting an illness like cancer takes courage, determination and strength. It is not something a person should ever have to go through alone. Whether that person has a support system of family, friends or a combination, this group of people could easily be referred to as "teammates."

My hope is that this story might inspire someone to do a little extra for a person in their life who needs some support. Maybe it's simply stopping by to say hello … or maybe it's something that takes additional effort or a more significant commitment. The main thing is to let that person know he or she is not alone.

Become a part of someone's "teammates for life" and you can make an enormous difference. It is an opportunity that you are fortunate to have … and it is an exercise that you will never regret.

CHAPTER 1

The Long Walk to McKale

There are specific moments in time that have a dramatic effect on a person's life. It is easy to look back later and see how life was markedly different before that moment ... as well as after.

That instance could be something subtle, like a decision to reach out with a kind word or gesture that lifts a person in need, causing a ripple effect that touches many.

Other times, a person knows with 100 percent certainty, right then and there, that this hour – on *this day* – will make all the difference. Like a grown man carrying another grown man over his shoulder under the heat of the Arizona sun, trying to find help for his ailing friend.

Monday, February 28, 2005 was one of *those* days.

A crowded parking lot near the McKale Center at the University of Arizona was nothing new in 2005. The Wildcats led the Pac-10 Conference in attendance at men's basketball games for the previous two decades as Coach Lute Olson had built one of the nation's top programs after his arrival in Tucson in the spring of 1983.

Coach Olson had achieved similar success in his prior job as the head men's basketball coach at the University of Iowa, where he worked from 1974-83, leaving as the Hawkeyes' all-time leader in victories.

At noon on this day – Monday, February 28 – a bright blue sky and sunshine overlook the parking lot as a navy blue sedan weaves around the corners, trying to locate a place to park. The pair of 47-year-old men in the car are two of Coach Olson's former players at Iowa, Mike "Tree" Henry and Kenny Arnold.

After finding a parking spot, the driver emerges from the car. Henry is an imposing figure – six-foot-nine and 285 pounds – wearing a white polo shirt and khaki pants. He walks around to the other side of the vehicle and opens the passenger door.

The lone passenger in the car is Arnold, who was diagnosed with a brain tumor in 1984, underwent brain surgery shortly thereafter and had suffered several strokes in the two decades since. His body has been ravaged, leaving him exhausted. Arnold, who measures six-foot-two, weighs only

135 pounds at the time, 65 pounds less than his weight as a college athlete. They fear that Arnold's cancer has returned. At this point, he is too weak to walk.

Henry leans over the car door to make eye contact with Arnold, and says to his friend simply, "I gotcha ... Let's go."

Henry lifts Arnold up over his left shoulder, braces himself for a second and begins to carry his former teammate across the parking lot. Even with the temperatures in the 80s, Arnold is wearing a black sweatshirt and jeans to keep his frail body warm.

As Henry carries his friend up about a dozen steps toward the arena, he feels sweat begin to pour down his forehead. He is heading to the basketball offices in the McKale Center, a place where he has never been before.

Halfway up the steps, Henry pauses to wipe the sweat from his face and catch his breath. Both men laugh quietly, perhaps due to nerves but also incredulous about their circumstances.

———————————

How did they get to this point, one man carrying another man over his shoulder to a basketball arena neither of them had seen before?

Henry and Arnold were teammates on the 1980 Final Four team at Iowa, coached by Olson. The 1980 team had a 25-year reunion in Iowa City planned for February 19, 2005 and the team would be recognized at Carver-Hawkeye Arena that day at halftime of the Iowa basketball game.

Arnold, living in Chicago with his mother at the time and struggling terribly with his medical issues, did not plan on attending. A proud man, Arnold didn't want his teammates and friends to see him in his weakened condition.

But one of his Hawkeye teammates, Ronnie Lester, felt that Arnold needed to be there. At the time, Lester – who was an All-American at Iowa – was the Assistant General Manager of the Los Angeles Lakers. He decided to fly into Chicago from Los Angeles, then drive to Iowa City and bring Arnold with him to the reunion. Lester wouldn't take "no" for an answer.

Lester – and all of Arnold's former Iowa teammates at the reunion – were shocked at how their friend appeared. His body was wasting away and his energy level was very low. Their overwhelming fear was that Arnold's cancer had returned and that he was likely not receiving the medical care that was necessary. "Everybody was concerned," said Lester. "These are all great guys and everyone wanted to know what they could do to help."

They felt that unless they did *something* at that moment, Arnold wouldn't survive much longer.

Coach Olson's Arizona team was playing UCLA on the Saturday of the 1980 team's reunion, so he was unable to attend. The players called their former coach – still trusting that he could guide them in the right direction as he had done so often 25 years earlier – and Olson was quick with an answer.

"He told us that he would pay for two tickets to have someone fly Kenny down to Tucson right away," said Henry. "And Lute would make sure the right people would see Kenny at the Cancer Center there. They would get to the bottom of it and do whatever they could to help."

Henry continues to carry Arnold on the long walk to the McKale Center.

"We didn't say anything on that walk to the arena," Henry said later. "But I know this much, I didn't want to let him down. Carrying Kenny up to the McKale Center was like running wind sprints in our basketball training ... you've got to do what you've got to do. So you just keep going."

When they enter the arena, Henry begins looking for the men's basketball offices. The 6-9 Henry carrying a grown man over his shoulder draws strange looks from each person they pass as they move along the concourse. "It had to be a bizarre scene for people who had no idea what was happening," said Henry.

There are women playing volleyball on the court at that time and one of the volleyball players yells up to Henry to see if they need help or a wheelchair. "No, I got it," Henry replies. And they just keep going, looking at names on doors, while a steady stream of sweat continues to drip from Henry's forehead.

After walking 180 degrees around the concourse circle, Henry arrives at the men's basketball office and enters. He helps Arnold into a seat and tells the secretary they are there to see Coach Olson.

Coach Olson and his staff are in a coaches' meeting. The Wildcats are rated ninth in the nation at the time with a 24-5 overall record. But they have just seen a seven-game winning streak come to an end two days earlier in a 93-85 loss at Washington. The staff is preparing for a battle with in-state rival Arizona State coming up on Saturday, March 5.

Arizona Assistant Coach Jim Rosborough, who had also worked with Coach Olson at Iowa, comes out of the meeting to see Henry and Arnold. He leads them back to the conference room to see Coach Olson. Henry lifts Arnold out of his chair, holds him around the waist and walks him into the conference room.

"Coaches Olson and Rosborough were shocked to see Kenny's physical condition," said Henry. "They got Kenny a chair and got him seated but then they weren't sure what to say. Lute and Ros gave me looks of concern."

Arnold tries his best to take some of the pressure off. "I'm OK," he tells the coaches. "It's good to see you guys."

"That was Kenny's attitude," said Henry. "He downplayed it ... he never wanted to be a bother and he didn't want to ask for help."

After exchanging a few pleasantries, Coach Olson says, "I'm glad you're here."

Coach Olson was in a unique position to help. His family had donated $1 million to the Arizona Cancer Center, it was announced only five weeks earlier on Monday, January 24. The endowment was created in the name of Coach Olson's first wife, Bobbi, who had died from ovarian cancer four years earlier.

Bobbi Olson was very much like a second mother to Coach Olson's players through the years. Both Henry and Arnold were close to her during their time as basketball players at Iowa.

During his wife's two-and-a-half-year battle with cancer, Coach Olson had become very familiar with the oncologists at the Arizona Cancer Center. "We have a great hospital here," said Coach Olson. "Dr. David Alberts, the Dean of the Cancer Center, has been a good friend for a long time. It's an unbelievable hospital and one of the top-rated cancer centers in the country.

"We told Tree to make sure to get Kenny down here and we'd take care of everything for him."

After they arrived in Tucson, Henry said the overriding thought he had was what to do next.

Thankfully, Coach Olson had prepared a plan for Arnold upon his arrival. "Lute told us the agenda," said Henry. "He told us exactly who we needed to see – and when – in the next couple of days at the hospital."

Henry said the biggest fear was not knowing what was going on and why Arnold's body was wasting away. "My thought was that it was cancer ... and it's bad," said Henry. "Kenny had already overcome so much, I was just hoping it wasn't too late to help him. But Coach Olson was going to put him in good hands."

The men visited for about a half-hour, catching up and talking about the Wildcats' season. The coaches were getting ready for their 1:30 p.m. practice that day.

"At the end of the discussion, we had to go find the doctor's offices and get checked in," said Henry. "They got us a wheelchair for me to take Kenny back out."

Those handful of days and tests in Tucson revealed both good and bad news about Arnold's health. "We were relieved to find out that the cancer had NOT returned," said Henry. "That was great to find out. But the bad news was that the facility in Chicago had been prescribing ineffective medication for Kenny that was causing parts of his body to atrophy and it would be impossible to correct the damage that had already been done.

"So, we were able to get him on some new meds that would help, but it was going to be a very uphill battle for Kenny physically. The scary thing is that, had we not had a reunion in Iowa City, had Ronnie not made the effort to bring Kenny and had Lute not stepped up ... I don't know how much longer Kenny could've lasted. It wouldn't have been long. But we were lucky and everyone did what they could to help."

Looking back now, Henry shakes his head and knows that February 28, 2005 was a day that made an enormous difference for Arnold. And for Henry himself. Along with so many others.

"People ask me 'How do you do these things?'" said Henry. "The answer is simple. Kenny is my brother, he's my teammate. That bond will never be broken."

They are teammates for life. And Arnold's team turned out to be even bigger than he realized.

CHAPTER 2

Adversity Provides Opportunity

It's December of 1979. I am a 10-year-old sixth grader, not quite five-feet tall with a skin-and-bones body. I spend most of my free time out on the driveway, shooting baskets at the hoop secured above the door of our one-car garage. Wearing a winter coat, Chicago Bears stocking cap, scarf and gloves doesn't stop me from working on my ballhandling and shooting. And dreaming.

I have big dreams. I want to be a basketball player for the Iowa Hawkeyes. For a kid in Iowa, there isn't anything much bigger or better than that.

So, I pretend to be the Hawks playing against whichever opponent is next on the schedule. I dribble up the court pretending to be Iowa's All-American point guard Ronnie Lester, then throw a pass over to a shooter like Kenny Arnold or Bobby Hansen ... and feed the ball to post players like Steve Krafcisin and Steve Waite. I might shoot a baseline jump shot, pretending to be Vince Brookins or Kevin Boyle ... and hustle after rebounds like I am Mike "Tree" Henry or Mark Gannon.

In my imaginary games, the scores are usually close ... but the Hawks almost always prevail in dramatic fashion. I keep the stats in my head and announce the games as they progress, building my imagination and sense for the dramatic finish. "Five seconds left ... the score is tied ... Lester drives ... THREE ... TWO ... he passes it to Arnold ... ONE ... he shoots ... it's GOOD! The Hawkeyes WIN!"

Over and over again.

Thud ... thud ... thud, thud, thud ... swish.

"The Hawkeyes win!"

———————————

I grew up in a family of 10 people: Dad, Mom, six boys and two girls. We lived in a Northeast Iowa town called Strawberry Point, which had a population of approximately 1,400 at the time. Our house had four bedrooms, three TVs and one shower. We had a 1974 Chevy Impala station wagon ... and Dad had a company van that we used when necessary. It seemed like we had it all.

There were no laptops, cell phones or the internet. We didn't even have a VCR at that point.

"The Jerk" and "Kramer vs. Kramer" were the top movies in late 1979, while "Happy Days," "Diff'rent Strokes" and "The Love Boat" were among the highest-rated TV shows. The top pop songs of that year included "My Sharona," "YMCA" and "I Will Survive."

Ted Koppel had recently become the anchor of a nightly news program about the U.S. hostages in Iran that would become the TV show "Nightline." And a guy named Ronald Reagan had just announced his candidacy for President.

In December of 1979, my oldest sibling – my sister Maggie – was 17. My youngest sibling was my brother Jerry, who turned four years old on December 20. I was the fifth of the eight children in my family and the fourth boy.

One thing people noticed about our family – besides the size of our crew – was that we were all very big sports fans. (Everyone except my younger sister Katie, who wanted nothing to do with sports and my recollection is that she spent 95 percent of her time in her room listening to Michael Jackson and Wham cassette tapes.) My three older brothers – Dan, Joe and Tim – taught me a lot about sports and the four of us taught my two younger brothers, Ed and Jerry.

When there was an Iowa Hawkeye football or basketball game being played, our house pretty much shut down. We would gather around the TV – or bring our "good radio" into the living room – and follow the game, cheering, agonizing and celebrating together.

Dad was always the most colorful with his reactions and commentary. At that time, he was 55 years old, but when an Iowa game was taking place, he might as well have been a teenager. During one basketball game, when an Iowa player missed a wide-open layup, Dad did a somersault in our living room, narrowly avoiding a collision with a coffee table. His language would occasionally grow more colorful, depending on the importance of the game. Mom was always there to rein him in as much as possible with comments like, "It's just a game!" But she was just as much into the Hawkeye games as we were.

The seven of us kids would sprawl out on the living room floor, eat popcorn, drink Pepsi and react to each score as if we were directly involved in the action. There were alternately high fives and fists pounding the shag carpet floor, depending on how the Hawks were faring.

Two days after Jerry's fourth birthday – December 22, 1979 – something happened that I would never forget.

It was a Saturday game, the Hawks were playing against Dayton in "The Dayton Classic" in Dayton, Ohio. Iowa was unbeaten (7-0) at the time and rated 13th in the nation. Our family was gathered around the radio in our living room. Dad was in his usual spot in his chair, while seven of us kids were gathered around on the floor. Mom was in and out of the room, working on something in the kitchen but never for more than a few minutes without checking in to find out the score.

There was a lot of excitement surrounding this basket-ball team, although at 10 years old, I thought it was normal. High expectations? *Why not?* I didn't know any better.

Iowa had won the Big Ten Conference title the season before (tied with national champion Michigan State and Purdue). The Hawks were led by point guard Ronnie Lester, who was All-Big Ten in 1978-79 as a junior and a Second-Team

All-American. Coach Lute Olson had successfully turned the program around after the Hawks had suffered four consecutive losing campaigns prior to the 1974-75 season when he took over.

This 1979-80 team had the makings of a team that could repeat as Big Ten champions and maybe even make a run at the national title, if everything went just right.

But that Saturday in Dayton, on December 22, things went wrong. Very wrong.

Lester drove to the basket and was undercut by a Dayton player. He landed awkwardly and injured his right knee. I remember all of us in our living room, staring at the radio as if waiting for an immediate diagnosis, but fearing the worst.

The Hawks won the game, improving their record to 8-0. But it was the emptiest of feelings after a victory that I can remember. It was clear that Lester would need to miss a large chunk of the rest of the season.

On December 23, Coach Olson and his staff had to figure out how to keep this Hawkeye team on the right path without its star point guard, who also happened to be the school's all-time leading scorer.

"Ronnie's injury was devastating because he was head-and-shoulders above everyone else on the team," said Jon Darsee, a sophomore reserve for that 1980 squad. "He was a strong leader and everything we did was built around our confidence in him."

Coaches talk a lot about facing adversity ... and how a person or team reacts to a negative situation shows a great deal about their character. This Iowa team was about to find out quite a bit about its true character. In fact, the Lester injury was only one situation the Iowa team had to deal with in a short period of time. Freshman forward Mark Gannon missed the second half of the season with a torn ACL in his knee, freshman guard Bobby Hansen had to play with a broken left hand, sophomore guard Kenny Arnold had a broken thumb on his right hand and Assistant Coach Tony McAndrews suffered serious injuries in an airplane crash on a recruiting trip.

It was an awful lot for anyone to handle, especially with the pressure of winning basketball games always at the forefront. Basketball Athletic Trainer and Travel Coordinator John Streif was working overtime just to keep a competitive team of student-athletes available for Coach Olson.

"I remember John Streif holding everybody together," said Gannon. "He wasn't just taping ankles. He was the glue who kept it all together. He told us to just keep moving forward ... and *keep going.*"

How was Streif able to help keep everyone's spirits high when the injuries kept piling up? "You take it day by day when adversity comes your way," said Streif. "You don't realize the magnitude of it at the time. It's not until you look back when it's all over that you see how impactful it is.

"Some of the greatest teams we had were maybe those that had the most adversity. I've always felt that injuries are a negative side of sports, but they provide an opportunity to learn and grow. Certainly, those guys on the 1980 team did that. We had the people and the character to get through it."

On December 23, the day after Lester injured his knee in Dayton, the question remained: Who would help the Hawks keep going by taking over the ballhandling, scoring and leadership responsibilities that were left wide open with Lester unable to play?

While the entire Hawkeye team pulled together and every player had to do a little bit more to make up for the loss of Lester, there was only one player who moved into Lester's position of starting point guard: Kenny Arnold.

"There was no question that Kenny could keep things afloat for us," said Coach Olson. "The other players really respected Kenny and the way he played."

"Coach Olson did a great job of rearranging personnel and Kenny was the guy," said Kevin Boyle. "Moving Kenny to point guard was the biggest transition of the year."

"Every year, Kenny got better," said Lester. "You could see it. And you knew he was ready. His first year was a learning experience."

Arnold was a sophomore and like Lester, he was a Chicago native. The two guards were the same height at 6-2, but Lester had elite speed and quickness, with the ability to stop on a dime and raise up for his shot. Lester was an All-Big Ten guard the season before, along with Michigan State's Magic Johnson.

Arnold was the type of player some might have described as "good at everything, but not elite at anything." Except those people wouldn't have known Arnold's toughness, determination, leadership and poise. These were the elite traits that Arnold had all along, along with his intelligence on the basketball court.

"Kenny was one of the sharpest players I ever coached," said Assistant Coach Jim Rosborough, who has coached at the collegiate level for 39 seasons. "He had a very high basketball IQ."

Arnold, who scored only 50 points as a freshman at Iowa the entire season before, was suddenly thrown into the role of quarterbacking a veteran team that everyone expected to win. The kid from Chicago was ready for the challenge.

"Ronnie and Kenny were two really different types of players," said Gannon. "But even though Kenny was a different style of player, he adapted quickly, he protected the ball and he saw the floor really well. And he never missed a free throw under pressure."

"Ronnie was our main guy, but we were such a close-knit group, with great team chemistry," said Steve Waite. "We absolutely had confidence in Kenny. He showed it every day in practice. When you're going against Ronnie every day in practice, you're going to learn a lot of things and become pretty good."

Arnold finished the season with averages of 13.5 points, 4.3 assists and 3.5 rebounds per game. In 33 games played, he scored the most points on the team (444) and handed out the most assists (142).

"Kenny Arnold should've been Player of the Year in the Big Ten Conference that season," said Rosborough. "Under the circumstances, filling in for Ronnie Lester, playing with a broken thumb and then performing as well as he did. We wouldn't have been anywhere without Kenny."

"Kenny was a master, a wizard the way he took care of the ball," said Waite. "He could handle the ball, see the floor, pass it quickly and he was a very good shooter. He was so impressive."

With Lester sidelined, the Hawkeyes struggled to a 2-4 start to the Big Ten season. But thanks in large part to Arnold's steady play at point guard, the Hawks managed to finish the conference season with a 10-8 mark, which gave the team a 19-8 record. Their 19 victories were just enough to earn an invitation to the NCAA Tournament and with Lester returning to the lineup – although slowed a great deal due to his knee injury – the Hawks felt they could make some noise in the tourney.

"We went through a lot of adversity that year," said Lester. "But we were tough. We knew what it took to win games."

––––––––––

A large part of the Hawkeyes' toughness as a team could be attributed to Coach Olson's focus on fundamentals, details and discipline at both ends of the court. "That was back in the years of two-and-a-half-hour practices," said Krafcisin. "You'd run until you can't run anymore. We were all incredibly competitive and we wanted to win. But we also didn't want to deal with Lute if we played bad."

Krafcisin recalled one victory against a non-conference opponent that was closer than it should've been due to some sloppy execution by the Hawks. "When Coach came into the locker room after the game, he just said 'Bring your running shoes tomorrow' and nothing else ... and the balls didn't come out at the next practice," said Kraficisin. "He had high expectations for us and wanted us to be fundamentally sound, take care of the ball and compete."

Krafcisin, who has spent his professional career coaching college basketball, has earned more than 300 victories as the head coach for the Des Moines Area Community College women's basketball program. He learned a great deal from Coach Olson about what it takes to be a successful coach. "Lute had incredible attention to detail with fundamentals," he said. "I can still hear him repositioning me on post-ups, how to feel the defender on a reverse pass, how to V-cut, how to get open. Lute gave us that attention to detail."

While Coach Olson was focused on details and discipline, he managed to also set the tone for decorum.

"Lute commanded the respect," said Hansen. "He always had the right words to get you going ... and he never swore."

I remember the day the 1980 NCAA Tournament pairings were announced. My brothers and I were all watching TV together, waiting for the information. But I fell asleep on the living room floor.

When I woke up, I wanted to know two things: Did the Hawks make it? If so, who were they going to play?

My older brothers answered that yes, Iowa made the tournament. And the Hawks would be playing Virginia Commonwealth in their opening game. I didn't believe them. "Virginia Commonwealth sounds made up," I said. At 10 years old, I must have been expecting a more marquee name like UCLA, Kansas State or Marquette. I waited for confirmation later and found out that Virginia Commonwealth was, indeed, a college … and VCU would be Iowa's first-round opponent in the 1980 NCAA Tournament. The Hawks were a 5-seed in the East Region.

"We had all the faith in the world in Kenny, but it was great going to the NCAA Tournament with Ronnie back," said Krafcisin. "When Ronnie was out there playing, he was so good, it made everything easier. When he was hurt, we all had to shoulder the burden a bit without him, but it made us better. When the tournament started, it was almost like Christmas for us, because now our team was better, Kenny was better and Ronnie was back."

On Thursday, March 6, Iowa defeated VCU 86-72 in the first-round game in Greensboro, North Carolina. Arnold scored 23 points to lead five Hawks in double-figures. The others included Lester (17), Boyle (17), Waite (17) and Krafcisin (10).

Krafcisin had played for Coach Dean Smith and North Carolina prior to transferring to Iowa in the fall of 1978. "A lot of fans in Greensboro were giving him a hard time," said Gannon. "Krafcisin was so nervous that he got sick in the locker room. While Coach Rosborough was giving the scouting report before the game, Steve went back to the toilet to throw up. Coach kept going, 'Steve, you're going to guard so-and-so, can you hear me back there?'

"And Steve yelled back, 'Yeah ... I got it.' Then we could hear him throw up again. But he was such a gamer. Once he smelled the popcorn, he could really play." Krafcisin finished that victory with 10 points, nine rebounds and five assists. The 6-10 center remains the only player in college basketball history to play and score in Final Fours for two different teams.

"Once we got in the tournament and won our first game, we felt that we were peaking right then and playing great ball," said Waite. "Our confidence really started to build. Plus, our coaches were very good at game planning. You see the difference between coaches and teams that are well-prepared and those that just have great talent. We might not have been the most talented team, so the coaching staff's game planning and preparation was critical for us."

The Hawks faced North Carolina State on Saturday, March 8 in the second round and it figured to be a much tougher game. Sidney Lowe, Thurl Bailey and Dereck Whittenburg

21

were all freshmen for NC State and they would win the national title three years later, but on this day, it was a Hawkeye victory, 77-64. Arnold led the way again with 18 points, while Lester and Vince Brookins each scored 17.

Iowa was executing extremely well at the right time of the year. "Coach Olson is a great coach and he had a great staff," said Lester. "We were always prepared and always in great condition. Coach Olson is always organized and knows what he wants done."

"Coach Olson had a really good game plan for every game we played," said Gannon.

The Hawks would need another good game plan the following Friday, March 14, as they were matched up with top-seeded Syracuse – coached by Jim Boeheim – in a game at The Spectrum in Philadelphia, Pennsylvania. The Hawkeyes prevailed again, 88-77, with another team effort. Five players scored in double-figures: Brookins (21), Boyle (18), Krafcisin (14), Arnold (12) and Waite (10). Lester finished with nine points and seven assists, while freshman Hansen came off the bench to total four points and three assists.

"We handled Syracuse pretty good," said Hansen, who later won an NBA title with the Chicago Bulls in 1992. "Then we thought we couldn't lose. Our confidence was sky high."

This victory set up a showdown with Georgetown and Coach John Thompson in a battle to get to the Final Four, the biggest stage in all of college basketball. The entire state of Iowa seemed to be locked into cheering for this Hawkeye team.

Iowa would be underdogs, but it was a role this team had gotten familiar with and maybe even embraced. "We didn't get a lot of respect," said Krafcisin, adding that people would get Iowa confused with Idaho ... or Ohio. "We had a scripted 'I' on the side of our game shorts that looked like a corncob and we'd take crap about being 'the kids of the corn.' But we took a lot of pride in what we were doing and that helped fuel us."

I remember saying to myself the day after the victory over Syracuse that I would not get too upset if Iowa lost to Georgetown. I figured that the Hawks would get to the Final Four sometime in the next two or three years ... and that would be good enough for me. At 10 years old, I figured this kind of success on the basketball court happened all the time.

On Sunday, March 16 at The Spectrum, the Hawks trailed Georgetown by 10 points at halftime, but showed incredible determination and grit by playing a nearly perfect second half. Coach Olson's team made 17 of its last 21 field-goal tries and all 15 of its second-half free throws to beat the Hoyas 81-80 to earn a spot in the Final Four.

Waite made a three-point play with a few seconds remaining to give the Hawks the victory, but there were several heroes for Coach Olson's team on this day. Brookins stayed hot with his shooting to lead Iowa with 22 points. Waite finished with 15 points, while Boyle had 14 and Arnold 12 for the victors. Lester had eight points and nine assists, while Hansen had eight points without missing a shot.

This would be Iowa's first trip to the Final Four since losing to San Francisco and Bill Russell in the championship game in 1956, which was 24 years earlier.

"I get reminded about that game a lot," said Waite. "People can tell me exactly where they were when that play happened. I think that's awesome. I'm very proud to be a part of that team. And against Georgetown, it wasn't just us playing well ... when you look at the shooting percentages and turnovers for *both* teams, it was unbelievable. Probably one of the greatest showcases of that sport ever. We were just fortunate to have the ball at the end."

Waite was correct about the efficiency of both teams that day. Georgetown made 33 of 55 shots from the floor (60 percent) and 14 of 16 free throws (88 percent), while Iowa made 31 of 51 shots from the floor (61 percent) and 19 of 20 free throws (95 percent).

"Georgetown beat us up pretty good the first half," said Lester. "But there was something about our team and our coaching staff. We were always going to play to the end. It was really two different games that day ... but we played almost error-free basketball in the second half."

When the Hawkeye team's flight landed in Cedar Rapids that Sunday night, after the victory over Georgetown, the team was in for a surprise.

"At some point on the flight home, we were told 'There's a lot of people waiting for you when you get back,'" said Henry. "When we arrived in Cedar Rapids, there were fans everywhere at the airport. It was crazy. Then, on the bus to Iowa City, there were people lined up on both sides of the highway all the way back."

When the team finally arrived in Iowa City about 20 minutes before midnight, almost 15,000 fans were waiting at The Iowa Field House to welcome them home. It was probably the largest pep rally in the state's history.

"Oh my God … it was unreal," said Henry. "I was almost speechless to see that crowd and that reaction. It is still one of the best memories of my life."

"It was unbelievable," said Brookins. "At The Field House, it was like it was noon instead of midnight. Even when we weren't very good, the Iowa fans were great, but that was just crazy. You couldn't even dream that up. I think that feeling even trumped preparing for the Final Four. Everybody was there in Iowa City lifting us up."

"The Iowa fan base was phenomenal, but when the popularity *really* hit was that pep rally," said Coach Rosborough. "I've never seen anything like it, before or since."

"The Iowa wrestling team had just won the national title and they were there too," said Boyle. "It was a great atmosphere and a great moment in Iowa history. Everybody who was there will remember that for the rest of their lives."

"Everyone knows that Iowa fans are above and beyond, but that was borderline crazy," said Gannon. "The fire marshal must have been out of town that weekend. I just remember thinking 'this is unbelievable.'"

Hansen said that the impromptu pep rally really brought home the magnitude of the team's accomplishment, earning a trip to the Final Four. "You could see the wide-eyed wonderment in everybody's eyes that night," he said. "The reality of what we had achieved was sinking in."

Coach Olson was handed a microphone to speak to the crowd and he asked, "Don't you people know that it's a quarter-to-12, for crying out loud?" The crowd erupted as the players, standing behind Olson, laughed. Olson's wife Bobbi, standing next to the coach, checked her watch and smiled. "Well, we've said all along that the Iowa fans are the greatest fans in the world," Coach Olson continued. "And this makes it official." Another ovation from the Hawkeye crowd ensued.

Lester, who went on to win an NBA championship as a player and six more titles as an executive with the Los Angeles Lakers, still holds this moment – and his years in Iowa City – in extremely high regard. "Iowa fans are the best," he said. "All these people at the airport, all these people lining the streets, then we walk into The Field House and it was full. I've said it before … my years at Iowa were probably the best four years of my life."

A few of the players took the microphone to speak to the crowd that night at the pep rally, including Arnold, who said, "I'm not much of a speaker, but I'd like to thank all the fans for the great support we've had this year." The crowd cheered and Arnold, wearing his black Iowa letter jacket, paused before delivering the best line of the night, "I hope to see you all out there at Market Square Arena this Saturday because the Hawks are going all the way!"

The crowd went absolutely crazy.

Iowa played Louisville at Market Square Arena in Indianapolis on March 22, 1980. The Cardinals were led by All-American Darrell Griffith, also known as "Dr. Dunkenstein" because of his leaping ability.

The Hawkeyes came out slow, but battled tough, and trailed 22-17 when the worst scenario for Iowa unfolded. The Hawks' All-American Lester had not missed a shot, scoring Iowa's first 10 points, when he re-injured his right knee on a drive to the basket. He was done for the day. As he headed to the bench, so did Iowa's chances for a national title.

"When Ronnie got hurt against Louisville, most teams would've crumbled but we played tough and kept battling," said Krafcisin.

Coach Olson's team fought like crazy to stay in the game and it was within a basket a few different times in the second half. Unfortunately, Louisville's Griffith was simply too much for the Hawks to handle, scoring 34 points in an 80-72 victory for the Cardinals.

Arnold scored 20 points to pace the Iowa team, while Brookins (14), Krafcisin (12) and Lester (10) rounded out the double-figure scorers for the Hawks.

Two days later, Louisville defeated UCLA, 59-54, to win the national championship.

"Coach Olson, Coach Rosborough and the staff were great at game planning," said Hansen. "We were always confident that we were prepared. When we went to the Final Four, we believed we could win it. And Ronnie was on fire against Louisville before he got hurt. It was always interesting to watch Ronnie's preparation, knowing that he was a future NBA guy, kind of like how I felt with the Bulls watching Michael Jordan prepare.

"That loss to Louisville was the most devastating loss of my basketball career."

Iowa fans still wonder, "What if Ronnie Lester had not been undercut at Dayton, Ohio in December of 1979? What if Lester had not re-injured that knee in the Final Four? Would Iowa have won the national title in 1980?"

But what is never in question is this: That 1979-80 Iowa basketball team overcame the odds, stuck together and competed like crazy to get the most out of its potential.

Hawkeye fans – including the Gallagher family in Strawberry Point – were in love with the Hawkeye basketball program. We felt like we knew the coaches, players and heck, even trainer John Streif, personally ... and we couldn't wait for the next season to begin.

Little did we know that the popularity of the Iowa basketball program was about to explode to new levels the following season.

CHAPTER 3

Hawkeyes Become TV Stars

The success of the 1980 Iowa basketball team left the Hawkeye fan base thrilled and wanting more.

Hawk fans had suffered through some very lean years in the 1970s in men's basketball and in the 1960s and 1970s in football. They were starving for something to get excited about ... and more than ready to go all in for Coach Olson's basketball program.

Another factor was that the state of Iowa was suffering through the midst of a major farm crisis. Exports had fallen, partially due to the 1980 U.S. grain embargo against the Soviet Union. Rising farm debts, falling prices of commodities, high interest rates and a record number of foreclosures had left much of the state in an economic mess.

The people of Iowa wanted something – *anything* – to feel good about. And heading into the fall of 1980, the Hawkeye basketball program was it.

Several of the key players from the run to the Final Four were returning for the Hawkeyes as they entered the 1980-81 season. The seniors included: Brookins, a 6-6 forward with a sweet jump shot; Henry, a 6-9 forward who was a fan favorite from the minute he arrived in Iowa City as a freshman in the fall of 1977; and Greg Boyle, a 6-2 guard who had played sparingly his first three years at Iowa.

Lester, Iowa's All-American guard, was gone. Even though he missed 15 games his senior season, Lester was the program's all-time leader in points (1,675) and assists (480) at that time. Lester was the 10th overall pick in the first round of the 1980 NBA Draft – he would be considered a "lottery pick" today – and started his career with the Chicago Bulls.

Despite the departure of Lester, the Hawkeyes had gained so much valuable experience the season before when Lester was injured that hopes were high among Hawkeye fans that the team could put together another terrific season.

———————————

Behind the scenes, something had taken place that would change things dramatically for the Iowa basketball program in the decade of the 1980s.

The Hawkeye basketball players were already basket-ball stars in the state of Iowa. They were about to become *TV stars*, too.

Bill Bolster, who was the General Manager at KWWL-TV in Waterloo, approached Iowa's Athletic Director Bump

Elliott about the creation of the Iowa Television Network in 1980. The idea was to broadcast Iowa basketball games state-wide because of the intense – and growing – fan interest in the Hawkeye program.

In 1980, the Iowa Television Network broadcasted six of the Hawkeye games. The games were shown on NBC affiliates located in Sioux City, Des Moines, the Quad Cities and Waterloo/Cedar Rapids, and a CBS affiliate in Mason City. For advertisers, this combination of stations created the 12th-largest market in the nation.

"At first, Bolster said 'Let's try putting six games on TV,'" said Coach Olson. "Then, of course, EVERY game was on TV."

The play-by-play announcer was 26-year-old Bob Hogue, who was KWWL's Sports Director. "I know that Bolster had a tough time convincing Bump Elliott that it was OK to televise home games," said Hogue. "Bump was worried that it would hurt the attendance. That's probably why we only did six games in 1980."

Not only did the TV exposure not hurt the gate at Iowa games, it drove the Iowa fans' passion for the Hawkeyes to a new level.

"Bill Bolster was very aggressive and a true visionary in the industry," said Hogue. "We were so ahead of other stations around the country at that time."

The success of the 1980 Hawkeye team – and the ratings for the games that were televised – led the new Iowa Television

Network to broadcast almost every game the remainder of the decade to a statewide audience. Every Thursday night at 7 p.m. and every Saturday afternoon at 1 p.m., you could count on most households in Iowa stopping for two hours to watch the Hawkeyes.

People scheduled their winter events around the Iowa games.

"Here's how popular those games were," said Hogue. "I heard more than once that when Iowa games were on TV on Thursday nights, the Highway Patrol would take their cars off the road because nobody was out driving." Whether that's true or not may be beside the point that Iowans could hear that statement and believe that it *might* be true.

"We used to hear stories that an old person would be very sick in the hospital but would say 'I'm going to wait to die until after I watch the Iowa game,'" said Coach Rosborough.

And there was no competition at the time from cable networks stealing the entertainment thunder, either. ESPN was still finding its legs and the Big East and ACC games were a couple of years away from capturing a national TV audience.

The ratings went through the roof. "We were getting 50 and 60 shares for those games back then," said Hogue. "That means that 50 to 60 percent of households in Iowa with TV sets turned on were tuned into those games. That's unheard of."

In fact, NBC allowed the Iowa affiliate stations to push back the network's Thursday night lineup ... and broadcast those shows on Sunday afternoons in the 1980s because

Iowa basketball games just crushed the ratings. Those shows that were shifted to Sunday afternoons included some of the top-rated TV shows in the country like "The Cosby Show," "Family Ties," "Cheers" and "Night Court," which were receiving somewhere between a 15 to 24 share.

The best night of TV shows on NBC simply couldn't come close to competing with the audience in Iowa for Hawkeye basketball. A 60 share versus a 20 share? Incredible.

The numbers are astounding. And quite telling about the popularity of Iowa basketball. "It was a perfect moment," said Hogue. "There were very few places in America that this perfect storm could occur and explode like this. One, there was a growth of live sports on television. Two, the passion of the state for the University of Iowa athletics was so great. And three, Lute had a really good team."

Bolster, a native of Waterloo who went on to become the Chairman and CEO of CNBC International, remembers those days fondly. "It was the neatest thing that I ever did and nothing else ever came close," he said. "Aggregating the Iowa basketball program for the entire state to watch the games at the same time together ... and then talk about the next day, it was wonderful. It was the greatest accomplishment in my craft that I ever achieved."

One key move that Bolster made before the 1980-81 season was hiring Ed Piette from a station in Detroit. "Ed had produced Detroit Tigers baseball, so he had the expertise of producing sports," said Bolster.

Piette also had experience with pregame shows and saw the potential that a 30-minute pregame show could bring to the Iowa basketball telecasts. "'Hawkeye Close-Up' was a pregame show that really brought the players and coaches into the home for the fans," said Piette. "It was cool to bring Lute, Bobbi and the team to life."

Diane Carraway, who was a host on the syndicated show "PM Magazine" for KWWL, did feature stories for "Hawkeye Close-Up" and Hogue would interview players and coaches. The ratings for the pregame show were terrific and created even more advertising opportunities for the Iowa Television Network. Plus, the fans began to feel like they really *knew* the people in the Iowa basketball program.

"Knowing the good that you could do with the pregame show was very important," said Bolster. "It was the opportunity to introduce *personality*."

And it didn't hurt that Coach Olson was a young, handsome, successful coach. "Lute was the perfect television coach," said Bolster. "Not just in appearance, but in demeanor. He looked like what Iowa wanted."

"Lute could not go anywhere without being mobbed, almost like seeing someone from Hollywood," said Carraway.

"And all of that came through the TV ... Iowans fell in love with him," added Piette.

It was a perfect recipe, with the right team at the right time for the state of Iowa. "Generally speaking, we needed something to hang our hat on and that was it," said Bolster. "These players and coaches became part of the culture."

———————————

Ted Danson, Michael J. Fox and Bill Cosby were big television stars in the United States in the 1980s, no doubt. But the ratings in Iowa for Hawkeye basketball were three times greater than any of those actors' TV shows.

So imagine how well-known Coach Lute Olson was in Iowa … and how beloved the players like Arnold, Hansen, Boyle, Brookins, Henry, Waite, Gannon and Krafcisin had to be. These guys were the TV stars in Iowa at a level that was arguably not seen in any other state in the nation.

"I don't know if we could've been any more popular," said Brookins. "I don't know if I wanted to be recognized all the time, but as long as people were respectful, it was great. And we always felt the support."

"We felt like we were making people happy," said Boyle. "There were times that you didn't have the privacy you wanted, but you'd much rather have it that way than not have the support."

In the 1980s, the only TV show that could put up ratings numbers like Hawkeye basketball in Iowa was the Super Bowl. And while the Super Bowl took place once a year, the Iowa games took place *twice per week* during the season.

A story in The Des Moines Register on January 12, 1983 detailed that "the governor postpones his budget message to the state legislature until tomorrow. Objections from the lawmakers caused the postponement because of tonight's televised University of Iowa basketball game."

The Quad City Times had a story on February 17, 1983 that explained "a nursing home administrator calls television official to check out the tip-off time of the televised Hawkeye basketball game, so that the residents of the nursing home could schedule their nap times appropriately."

"It was just incredible," said Coach Rosborough. "Every single game was on TV and the whole state went wild. The players were heroes and they were all really good kids. They were adored from Davenport to Sioux City."

As a result, even after all the years have passed, Hawkeye basketball players in the 1980s have a very special place in the hearts and minds of Iowa fans. And its broadcasters.

"The memories of that time and that group are marked indelibly in my mind," said Hogue. "Those guys are in my heart. They really are."

Sports fans from Iowa – maybe especially student-athletes who grew up in that decade – can list their favorite Hawkeyes from the 1980s with ease. Names like Ronnie Lester, Bobby Hansen, Vince Brookins, Kenny Arnold, Steve Waite, Steve Krafcisin, Kevin Boyle, Michael Payne, Steve Carfino, Waymond King, Todd Berkenpas, Craig Anderson, Greg Stokes, BJ Armstrong, Roy Marble, Ed Horton, Brad Lohaus, Jeff Moe, Troy Skinner, James Moses and on and on.

Those guys were the TV stars in this state with a population of 3 million people. And they are still recognized today – three decades later – anytime they make an appearance in Iowa.

"I still hear from people today who tell me, 'Your team was my start to watching Iowa basketball,'" said Hansen.

"Lute was really good at keeping us in our little world," said Krafcisin. "So it was not until I got to be an adult – and live and work in Iowa – that I could understand what it meant to people and what people would do to watch the games. They would schedule their work shifts around Thursday nights and Saturday afternoons. Because of our youth, we didn't realize how magical it was.

"But we were good enough kids that people accepted us like family. When people would meet us, they felt like they already knew us."

The Hawks may not have felt much different in Iowa City because their home games were regularly sold out, but they noticed a big change when they traveled anywhere else in Iowa. "People all over the state recognized us and felt like they knew us," said Waymond King. "It was a wonderful experience ... feeling that kind of love and adulation from the people of Iowa. I cherished every moment of it without getting a big head about it. It was a magical time."

The popularity of those televised games also meant that the young play-by-play announcer, Hogue, had also become an instant "celebrity" in the state of Iowa.

"It overwhelmed me," said Hogue. "As a young sportscaster, I tried to get out in the community as much as possible to cover local games. Some time in the early 1980s, I walked into a high school gym and heard an explosion of noise ... and I wondered, 'Who's here?' Then I realized, *it was me*. That surprised me and I was embarrassed."

Hogue, currently the Commissioner of the PacWest Conference, felt that Coach Olson brought something unique to the program that Iowans appreciated. "Lute Olson was a phenomenal coach and a tremendous gentleman," said Hogue. "He walked into a room in a regal manner, always impeccably dressed. But he was always so focused and competitive. Determined to win."

Coach Olson's emphasis on teamwork stood out. "I used to think that there were better athletes on some of the other Big Ten teams, but you couldn't find a better TEAM than Iowa had," said Hogue. "Those players knew their roles, they played to the best of their abilities and they were deserving of all their success."

Was the fame too much at times? "It's not uncommon for coaches and players to be recognized and celebrated, but this was every day you were a rock star trying to get in and out of a concert," said Hogue. "Nobody felt that more than Lute, who was a private person. His popularity probably meant that he and his wife Bobbi could no longer go out to dinner because of their celebrity, but he was always accommodating."

———————————

Gannon shared a story about how he and Hansen discovered their popularity and fame in Iowa had reached a new level. "The summer after our freshman year, Bobby and I went up to my uncle's cabin at the Lakes (in Northwest Iowa)," said Gannon. "It was the middle of the week and we were just putzing around on a boat, going under the bridge from East Lake to West Lake. We had ballcaps on and probably no shirts. Two old fishermen spotted us and yelled, 'Holy smokes! That's Hansen and Gannon!' That's when you knew it was something else … when two old fishermen from Dickinson County knew who we were."

———————————

One of the most popular Hawks of the 1980s was Steve Carfino, a guard from Bellflower, California. "My first experience with Hawkeye fans was on my visit, when people were coming up to me on the streets and saying, 'Hey, you're the recruit from California, welcome to Iowa!'" he said. "Once on campus, we had a shirts-and-skins game at The Field House before the football game and 8,000 people showed up to watch us play. Wow!"

Carfino shared that Coach Olson taught him a valuable skill away from the court. "Lute showed me how to keep walking as I was signing autographs, so I could make it to where I was going," he said.

"The popularity was all I knew of living, going to school and playing in Iowa," said Carfino, who now lives in Australia. "I don't even try to explain how popular we were to people at home in California or here in Australia, they look at me like I'm making it up. My family didn't believe me until they came to visit me during basketball season.

"Once, I was coming back to campus after staying at a friend's house for a weekend. He said, 'Let's stop at this Pizza Hut' in a small town about two hours outside of Iowa City. I said, 'OK, but let's get it to-go' because I didn't want to get stuck there. He said, 'Don't be ridiculous, your ego is out of control.' So, we started to eat it there and 15 minutes later, the Pizza Hut was packed with people bringing Hawkeye merchandise to get it signed. It was unbelievable."

———————

Coach Olson became an extremely popular speaker throughout the small towns of Iowa, if your town was lucky enough to book him. After the 1981 basketball season, my dad was among the boosters at Starmont High School who were able to land Olson to speak at our athletic banquet that spring.

I was 11 years old and attended that event with my parents, and my brothers Dan (a junior at Starmont), Joe (a freshman) and Tim (8th grader). We were excited to have Coach

Olson at our high school. It seemed almost surreal. Olson seemed like a statesman to me. He was tall, well-spoken, measured and his demeanor was what my mother would've described as "classy." He also had a full head of gray hair that was always perfectly combed.

Our high school was unique because it was six miles away from the nearest town. Starmont was made up of the students from three communities: Strawberry Point, Arlington and Lamont. The name Starmont was simply a combination of those three towns' names. The community members of those towns couldn't agree in which town to build the high school, so it was built in the middle of those towns, roughly six miles from each. You could look out the windows of your classroom and see nothing but cornfields.

Across the highway, though, was a small diner, the Maryville Café. I assumed it was popular among farmers and truck drivers, but I had never been inside. The night that Coach Olson came and spoke at Starmont was the first time I had entered the café.

About eight to 10 adults – along with Coach Lute Olson and his wife Bobbi – met at the café after the athletic banquet to engage in some conversation. It was heady stuff for the adults as they stood at the bar and likely grilled Coach Olson about all kinds of strategy questions and the expectations for the program going forward. It may not have been Olson's favorite thing in the world to do, but he was good at it. And the people of Iowa loved him.

At one point, I think Coach Olson was drawing out Xs and Os, explaining a specific strategy to our high school basketball coaches. A coaching clinic in a tiny café that was six miles from the nearest town. Only in Iowa.

As I recall, the four "Gallagher boys" were the only students in the place. We sat at a table with my mom and Bobbi Olson. We had never met Bobbi before that night, but she made us all feel like old friends within a matter of minutes.

Bobbi told us stories about the players and what fine young people they all were. She had a good sense of humor and her eyes smiled as she talked. Bobbi was friendly and engaging, and she answered every single question that my brothers and I could ask … and she appeared to be having as much fun as we were. Outside of my own mother, I thought she was the nicest woman I had ever visited with. We may have stayed there for 60 to 90 minutes before we had to leave because it was a "school night," but by that time, Bobbi had asked my brother Joe if he would be interested in being a caddy for Coach Olson at the Amana VIP Golf Tournament that summer in Iowa City.

Seriously. This was kind of unbelievable. Joe was thrilled to accept. Because my dad would take a few of us to that golf tourney every year at Finkbine Golf Course, Joe would be there anyway, so it was a done deal.

The Amana VIP was an extremely popular pro-am tourney, drawing some of golf's greatest players along with several celebrities, and on June 22, 1981, there were 20,000 fans who attended. In fact, that particular tournament included former

43

President Gerald Ford, who was playing in the Amana VIP for his third time.

But no matter who else was playing in that tournament, the fans were always fired up to see Coach Olson. We still have a photo of Tim and Joe standing at Olson's side as the coach signed autographs. Joe ended up riding around on a cart that day with Iowa's newest recruits, Michael Payne, Greg Stokes and Todd Berkenpas. Joe has a program from that tourney littered with autographs, including Payne, Stokes and Berkenpas, who would likely sign thousands of autographs in the next four years … and thousands more in the decades to follow. It was all a part of being a Hawkeye basketball star – as well as a TV star – in the state of Iowa in the 1980s.

Five years later at the Starmont High School athletic banquet, we had another member of the Hawkeye basketball family as our featured speaker. This time, it was 26-year-old Kenny Arnold. The emcee that evening was my brother Tim, who was 17 years old and only a few weeks from graduating. I was a 16-year-old junior and like everyone else in the room, I was excited to see the former Iowa basketball star in person.

Arnold spoke that night about perseverance and his own personal battle with cancer. He'd been diagnosed at a young age and had already been fighting for two years. He talked about the importance of staying positive regardless of the circumstances you're facing.

After the program, Arnold was sitting at a table on the stage, signing autographs and making small talk. The line was very long – more than 100 people – and moving slowly as everyone wanted to engage with him.

Suddenly, several police officers came running into the room. Our superintendent took the microphone and said something very brief like, "There has been an incident. We need you all to evacuate the building immediately."

Evacuate the building immediately? *What the ...?*

The police officers were scattering into the hallways. There seemed to be a dozen of them. Maybe more.

My family was there with my 83-year-old grandpa, Everett Stock, and our close family friend, 60-year-old Leo Gallagher (unrelated), who was completely blind. We weren't going to get anywhere very quickly. We did the best we could, however, to get the heck out of that building and head for home in Strawberry Point.

When we got home, we turned on the 10 p.m. news and tried to figure out what had just happened.

The initial story was that there had been an armed robbery at a bank in Oelwein late that afternoon. Oelwein was a town about 25 minutes from our school. The suspect had apparently called 911 and said that he was at the athletic banquet at Starmont High School and if they didn't come get him soon, he was going to open fire.

So, there was good reason for the commotion we had witnessed.

We worried about Arnold, who was the only African-American in the high school that evening in a crowd of a few hundred people or more. We were concerned for Arnold's safety and whether he returned to Iowa City without any issues. We wondered if this was a race-related incident ... or if it would be perceived as such.

The next day at school, our fears were quickly laid to rest.

As it turns out, there was a classmate of mine – a junior in high school – who was a big Hawkeye fan and wanted very badly to go to the athletic banquet that evening to see Arnold. But his parents didn't let him go. When he watched the 6 p.m. news on TV, he learned about the bank robbery in Oelwein. At some point that evening, he figured that if he couldn't be at the athletic banquet, then he was going to ruin it for everyone ... so he called the police with the made-up story about being the bank robber.

That was it. Arnold's evening at Starmont High School in 1986 was ruined because a teenage fan was upset about not being able to attend. Dozens of people who were waiting in line never got the chance to talk to Arnold or get an autograph. And Arnold must have believed the people from Starmont – the high school in the middle of cornfields – had to be crazy.

But that was the 1980s ... and that's how popular the Iowa Hawkeye basketball players were. Fame could be a wonderful thing, but it apparently had some warts, as well.

CHAPTER 4
Kenny and Tree

Kenny Arnold and Mike "Tree" Henry were born on the same day: June 7, 1959. It seems fitting that their lives have been tied together with such a strong bond since they became Hawkeye teammates in the fall of 1978, when they were 19 years old.

To better understand their connection, it helps to know a little bit about their individual backgrounds.

Arnold was born and raised on the South Side of Chicago, Illinois. The varsity basketball coach at Calumet High School, Johnie Butler, met Arnold on the neighborhood playground when Arnold was an 8th grader. "I was maybe 23 years old at the time," said Coach Butler. "I used to go to that playground to play. We had the older guys on one court and the 'wanna-bes' on the other court. Kenny was about 14 years old and maybe 6-1 at the time, but he could play."

Coach Butler said that Arnold was the center on his freshman team at Calumet, then he moved him out to the wing as a sophomore. "When he was a senior, I moved Kenny to the point," said Coach Butler. "He did well and we won our conference, which was very tough. Kenny had a classic shooting form and a feathery touch. Plus, he didn't back down from anything and always let his game do the talking."

It was Arnold's junior season, though, that made it clear to Coach Butler that Arnold could play at a high level in college. "We lost a close playoff game that year to Westinghouse, which had five future Division 1 college players: Mark Aguirre, Eddie Johnson, Bernard Randolph, Skip Dillard and Mike Jenkins," said Coach Butler. "Our team had Kenny, who was very good, and a good 6-3 forward named Alvin Johnson. All our other kids were six-foot or smaller. Kenny gave Westinghouse all it could handle. I talked to Mark Aguirre (who had a 13-year NBA career in which he averaged 20 points per game) later in life and he said that they were scared of our team that year, which meant to me that they were scared of *Kenny*."

Assistant Coach Jim Rosborough was the Iowa staff's lead recruiter for Arnold. "I saw him play a truckload of times in high school," said Rosborough. "And I never had any question that he could compete at the Big Ten level."

———————————

Arnold was more than a productive player at Iowa; he also became a leader. "Kenny lived two doors down from me and he was one of the guys I looked up to," said Michael Payne, who was a freshman in 1981-82 when Arnold was a senior. Payne had a tremendous rookie season for the Hawks, landing on Al McGuire's First-Team Freshman All-American Team along with Michael Jordan, Patrick Ewing, Keith Lee and Aubrey Sherrod.

"Kenny wasn't a vocal leader, but more by his actions and example," said Payne. "He was always calm and steady … never too up and never too down. He was a guide for me and the younger guys to follow."

Steve Carfino recalled what it was like learning from Arnold. "When I came on my official visit to Iowa, the Hawks' starting backcourt was Ronnie Lester and Kenny Arnold," said Carfino. "I remember thinking, 'Who calls the plays? Both of these guys are so quiet.'

"Well, I was nowhere near ready to start at the point for a Big Ten team, but I was a quick study and Kenny showed me how to earn the trust of Coach Olson and get more and more playing time."

Waymond King was also two years behind Arnold in school and he appreciated the example that Arnold set for the younger players. "Most guys in college, if they're good players, they tend to be more ego driven," said King. "But you never got that sense from Kenny. You knew when you played against him that you were going to have a hard time because he could flat-out play. Kenny was confident but not cocky. He had a workmanlike attitude."

He may have been a little quiet, but Arnold had a playful personality and loved to laugh. "His favorite musical group was George Clinton and Parliament/Funkadelic," said Waite. "We would be on a road trip and Kenny would have this big boombox and play 'We Want the Funk' a couple of times in a row. I would ask, 'Kenny, can't we get a little variety? Didn't they make any other songs?' And then he'd turn up the volume and play that same song 15 more times in a row. He would laugh and laugh. He was always laughing."

Arnold's roommate at Iowa all four years in Iowa City was Kevin Boyle, another Chicago native. "Off the floor, Kenny was a great all-around guy," said Boyle. "We got along so well."

Lon Olejniczak was a Hawkeye football player at that time but was a close friend of several of the basketball players, including Arnold. "Kenny was one of the funniest guys you could be around, but he was pretty shy," he said. "He was also one of the most unhealthy eaters I ever saw for as good an athlete as he was. He always had a double-burger with cheese, Honey Buns and a Coke."

Olejniczak recalled that Arnold's style was unique too. "Kenny was always in bell-bottom jeans, an Iowa t-shirt, his Iowa letter jacket, white high-top shoes and carrying around that boom box of his," he said, laughing. "He also always had a pick in his hair to fluff up his 'fro. He was 6-2 going on 6-6 with the 'fro, just like Fletch. He was losing it in the front, so he had to make up for it on top."

"Kenny made all of us laugh every day," said Carfino. "Every place we walked on campus turned into an impromptu tackle football game. If Kenny evaded a tackle, he would always celebrate with the Iowa State running back Dwayne Crutchfield touchdown celebration. It was funny every time, with leaves or snow in his hair, after taking a big hit.

"Maybe the funniest thing Kenny used to do was play the same song every day in the locker room when he arrived at practice, 'Christmas Rappin' by Kurtis Blow. It was a Christmas song and it was rap, back when rap was not popular with all walks of life, but because it was Kenny, we would all groan and then listen to the whole song."

Olejniczak summed up Arnold's personality with one more thought. "If I need to laugh or smile, all I've got to do is think about the time I spent with Kenny," he said. "I'll take that with me through the rest of my life."

At the end of his Hawkeye career, two things were clear about the guard who wore number 30 for the Black-and-Gold: Arnold was a winner and a clutch player.

Arnold produced at his highest level in Iowa's biggest games. During the 1980 NCAA Tournament, Arnold was Iowa's leading scorer with 17.3 points per game. During the Hawkeyes' first five games of the 1980 NCAA Tourney (not counting the meaningless consolation game), Arnold had an assist-to-turnover ratio of 19-to-three. He only made *three turnovers* in 181 minutes during that stretch of pressure-packed basketball.

This production and efficiency were not a surprise to Assistant Coach Tony McAndrews. "I can't remember ever telling Kenny to bust his butt," he said. "He always worked hard, had such a good temperament and was such a good guy. Kenny was very fundamentally sound."

Arnold played the second-most minutes in the NCAA Tournament of any player in Iowa history. The list of Hawkeyes who played 300+ minutes in the "Big Dance" is a short one: Kevin Boyle (354), Arnold (350), Roy Marble (346) and Bobby Hansen (304). Even more impressive is that in the nine NCAA Tournament games that Arnold played in as a sophomore, junior and senior, he averaged 37.8 minutes per game.

During two NCAA Tourney games, Arnold never left the court. In three others, he only sat for one minute apiece.

A clutch shooter, Arnold shot 52 percent from the field and 78 percent from the free-throw line during the 10 NCAA Tourney games he played in for the Hawks.

Always a winner, the Iowa teams that Arnold played on finished 85-33 overall (72 percent) and 48-24 in the Big Ten Conference (67 percent). Arnold's teams were 46-8 in Iowa City (85 percent). He played on one Big Ten championship team and two teams that finished second. Consistency and excellence were hallmarks of Arnold's Iowa career.

Mike "Tree" Henry was raised in Grambling, Louisiana, along with his sister Nannette. They were the children of Dr. Charles Henry and his wife Jeanette. Dr. Charles Henry served as the Chairman of Grambling State University's College of Health, Physical Education and Recreation from 1958 to 1974. He also served as Executive Officer and Secretary-Statistician for the Southwestern Athletic Conference from 1968 to 1973.

Mike Henry grew up with one nickname after another. His actual name is Charles Henry III. But because his mother was an art teacher, his friends began calling him "Little Mike" as a nickname, short for Little Michelangelo. "Little Mike" was later shortened to just "Mike." As he grew older – and taller – his friends nicknamed him "Tree."

Iowa fans have always known him as Mike "Tree" Henry.

With his father working closely with the Athletic Department at Grambling State, "Tree" was around some world-class athletic talent as a youngster in Grambling, a small town with a population of approximately 4,400 people.

"I was around the football players at Grambling a lot," said Henry. "These guys were not just great college players, but so many of them dominated at the professional level. Guys like Willie Brown, Buck Buchanan, Willie Davis, James Harris and Charlie Joiner. In fact, the person who taught me how to shoot a basketball was Coach Eddie Robinson." Robinson was the legendary football coach at Grambling, who at one point, was the winningest college football coach of all time with more than 400 victories.

Henry was around basketball greatness, as well. "The New York Knicks won the NBA championship in 1970 in the Game 7 that Willis Reed came on the floor after being injured and the Madison Square Garden crowd went crazy," said Henry. "A few days later, that same Willis Reed was at Grambling in the gym shooting baskets with me. I was 11 years old and shooting hoops with the NBA's MVP. It was incredible, but that's the way it was."

In 1974, Dr. Charles Henry was hired by Big Ten Conference Commissioner Wayne Duke to become the nation's first African-American to serve as Assistant Commissioner of any major college athletic conference. The job took the Henry family to Chicago where "Tree" Henry attended Larkin High School in Elgin, a suburb on the northwestern edge of Chicago.

Both of Henry's parents went to grad school at the University of Iowa, so his parents already had an affinity for the school and community when their son was being recruited in high school. "I'd been to Iowa City so many times with my dad on visits, I knew the university very well," said Henry.

———————

When Henry first arrived in Iowa City as a student-athlete in the fall of 1977, he unpacked his things and headed over to The Field House to shoot some baskets. "The first person I met at The Field House was former Hawkeye Larry Parker, whose final season with Iowa was in 1976," said Henry. "He was shooting by himself, so I introduced myself and we hit it off. Larry kind of took me under his wing and we became good friends."

Larry Parker and his wife at the time, Sara Parker, had three children and Henry remained a good friend of the family. The Parkers' youngest child was a girl named Candace. "My sister Nannette and I bought a crib for Candace when she was born," said Henry.

When Henry became an AAU girls' basketball coach in Chicago from 1999 through 2017, Candace Parker was one of his best players. "Mike would drive 45 minutes to practice a couple of times per week," said Sara Parker. "His time, energy and effort were so great, especially without having a girl on the team. Candace thought he was really nice and it was good to have a 6-9 guy to learn to shoot over. Mike donated a lot of time to coaching and there was nothing holding him there other than our friendship."

Candace Parker went on to star at the University of Tennessee where she won national titles in 2007 and 2008, earning National Player of the Year honors both seasons. Then Parker, who stands 6-4, became the first WNBA player to earn Rookie of the Year and MVP in the same season in 2008.

She has become one of the greatest women's basketball players of all time, averaging 17.5 points and 8.7 rebounds during an 11-year career with the Los Angeles Sparks. Parker is also a studio analyst during the NCAA men's basketball tournament for Turner and CBS. In addition, she became the first full-time, in-studio, female analyst for the NBA on TNT.

Other future WNBA players who Henry coached in AAU basketball include Morgan Tuck, Kaela Davis and Linnae Harper. "Tuck, Davis and Harper were on the Illinois Central Elite 12-and-under team that won the AAU national championship in 2007," said Henry, who coached that team to the title.

––––––––––––––––

Henry and Arnold first met in the summer of 1977. "We both went to Iowa's Elite basketball camp that summer before my senior year," said Henry. "In fact, I met several of the guys who I would play with at Iowa at that camp. Kenny was there, and so were Vince Brookins, Steve Waite and Kevin Boyle."

Arnold's high school coach said that Arnold made an impression on Iowa's coaching staff at that camp. "Kenny really enjoyed it and played well," said Coach Butler. "That's when Coach Olson and Coach Rosborough really started recruiting him. (Indiana Coach) Bobby Knight made some overtures and so did Tennessee, but Kenny was pretty comfortable with picking Iowa."

Henry and Arnold got together again a few months later. "I hosted Kenny on his unofficial visit to Iowa that fall and we hit it off instantly," said Henry. "He was laid back so we had similar personalities. We also had a similar interest in music. When he committed to Iowa and came to campus in 1978, we were pretty inseparable."

While Henry's basketball career at Iowa didn't provide him with as many opportunities for playing time as he would've liked, the power forward with the easy smile was a crowd favorite from the very beginning.

When the Hawkeyes would have a double-digit lead in a home game at The Field House in the final minutes, the crowd would begin to chant "TREE!" in unison … attempting to coax Coach Olson into putting Henry in the game.

One mythical story – that has been re-told so many times it has almost become true – is that one game, Coach Olson told Henry to check in at the scorer's table. Henry was so excited that he stood up, pulled down his warm-up pants, but also pulled down his uniform shorts at the same time. Legend has it that Henry was standing there in his jockstrap for all 13,365 fans at The Field House to see.

"I was really skinny, so I had my sweatpants tied very tight," said Henry, laughing at the mention of the story. "This was before 'tear-aways,' so when I pulled my sweatpants down, I started to grab my shorts too. They didn't come down very far. One sportswriter noticed … and the legend has grown."

One story that didn't need any embellishment took place on the campus of a rival Big Ten school. "In the fall of 1979, Kenny and I were at Northwestern University in Evanston, taking a friend of ours to school there and helping him get moved in," said Henry. "While Kenny and I were walking around campus there, we ran into Michael Wilbon. Kenny had known Michael for some time as they grew up in the same neighborhood and knew each other in high school.

"Kenny introduced me to Michael and said, 'This guy is going to be a great writer someday.'" Wilbon, of course, went on to become a legendary sportswriter and columnist for The Washington Post ... and then became a television personality for ESPN as the co-host of "Pardon the Interruption" and a regular contributor on other shows, as well.

Bobby Hansen has been Iowa's basketball analyst on its radio broadcasts since 1993. "A few years ago, Michael Wilbon walked across the gym at Northwestern and asked me how Kenny was doing," said Hansen. "He told me how much he looked up to Kenny when they were younger."

––––––––––––

Henry was one of the very few Iowa players who had his own car in their college days, a brown 1974 Maverick. "I used to ride around quite a bit with Kenny, Vince and Mike Henry," said Waite. "Tree usually drove. We'd be going by cornfields and farmland, and Kenny would always get at me because I'm from Iowa. There would be cows out in a pasture and Kenny would say, 'Hey Waiter, what are those ... DAWGS?' And he'd laugh and laugh."

"We would have five or six of us pile into Tree's car," said Payne. "All of us would be 6-5 or taller, stuffed into that car. We'd park over at the mall and come out of that thing like spiders ... it had to be quite a sight. But we had great camaraderie. We all really enjoyed hanging out together and spending time with each other."

"Tree used to look after Kenny in college too," said Carfino, a freshman on the 1980-81 team. "We used to tease Tree because he wouldn't let anyone else sit in the passenger seat of his car except for Kenny."

Lester remembers Arnold and Henry would often hang out with Vince Brookins, as well. "They were like the three stooges," said Lester. "They were always together and always goofing off, especially Kenny and Vince. When you saw one of them, the other two were right there. They were friends from the get-go."

After his eligibility ended in the spring of 1981, Henry stayed at Iowa for another year and served as a student assistant in 1982, which was the senior season for Arnold. Both Henry and Arnold graduated from the University of Iowa in May of 1982.

The 1982 regular season ended in heartbreak for Hawkeye fans. Iowa was in position to win its second Big Ten Conference championship in the last four seasons, with an 11-2 league mark with five games to play. But the Hawks struggled down the stretch ... and two atrocious officiating calls clearly cost Iowa a pair of games and the league title.

As a 12-year-old, I was aghast that professional referees could so brutally ruin a game, not once, but TWICE, in the final week of the season. It seemed beyond unfair, bordering on criminal, for many fans in the state of Iowa.

First, on Saturday, February 27, in a battle between the Big Ten's top two teams, Minnesota – led by Randy Breuer and Trent Tucker – matched up with the Hawks in The Field House. The game was a thriller that went into three overtimes. Apparently, that was enough for the officiating crew as they called a "phantom foul" against Gannon when the Gophers' Darryl Mitchell heaved a 35-foot desperation shot at the buzzer of the third overtime. Photos and replays revealed that Gannon never touched Mitchell. But as Mitchell drained the free throw after time expired, the outcome was sealed. Highway robbery, part one.

Then, one week later on Saturday, March 6, Iowa needed a victory at Purdue to tie Minnesota for the league championship. With no time remaining and the score tied at 65-65, official Jim Bain called a foul against Boyle, which would send the Boilermakers' Dan Palombizio to the free-throw line for the victory. Incredibly, replays would show that Boyle was nowhere near Palombizio on the play. In fact, the only Iowa player in the vicinity of the Purdue player was Greg Stokes. Boyle is a 6-6 Caucasian while Stokes is a 6-10 African-American, so it would be awfully difficult to mix those two guys up.

Coach Olson was so upset after the game that he said Bain's crew deserved "to be in jail." Not many Hawkeye fans would disagree with that assessment at the time.

I remember watching that game on TV and being so upset with how it ended. I couldn't believe what happened the week before, but AGAIN? Another "phantom foul" call with no time remaining? It seemed unfathomable. It made no sense to my 12-year-old self how the world could be so unfair. And without question, these two atrocious calls cost Iowa its second conference title in four seasons.

I wanted to cry, but felt I was too old for that. I wanted to swear, but I feared my parents' reaction. (The first time I swore in front of my parents was two years later on October 7, 1984 when Tim Flannery's ground ball went through Leon Durham's legs in Game 5 of the National League Championship Series.)

"As a team, we were disappointed," said Henry. "It was such a bad call at Purdue. Kenny got hammered on a couple of drives late and couldn't get a call. It hurts to have it taken out of your hands. But you just have to keep moving forward. As players, you shift your focus to the tournament and keep going."

After the unconscionably terrible officiating in the final week of the 1982 regular season, the Hawks suffered a 69-67 overtime loss to Idaho in the second round of the NCAA Tournament to end the season. Despite the heart-breaking last few weeks of that campaign, Arnold wrapped up his playing career at Iowa with some extremely impressive results, including:

During his four years, Iowa finished 1st, 4th, 2nd and 2nd in the Big Ten Conference.

Arnold scored 1,112 points.

He handed out 352 assists (9th all-time in Iowa history).

Arnold led the 1980 Final Four team in points and assists.

He played on Iowa's Big Ten championship team in 1979.

Arnold is second all-time in Iowa history for minutes played in the NCAA Tournament (350).

He is fourth in Iowa history for points scored in Final Four games (39).

Arnold is one of three players in Iowa history to score 20+ points in a Final Four game (Carl Cain and Bill Logan are the others).

The guard never left the court in the last game of his Iowa career, which went into overtime (45 minutes).

Arnold is one of six Hawkeyes to finish his career with at least 1,100 points, 350 assists, 250 rebounds and 80 steals.

After the 1982 season ended, Henry and Arnold went back to Chicago for a bit. "We went to the Big Ten office to see my dad one day," said Henry. "The Big Ten office, at that time, was flooded with mail from Iowa fans complaining about the terrible officiating and the calls that ruined our chance for another conference title. There was one office that was packed with boxes of these letters.

"Kenny and I were sitting there, in that office, reading some of the letters from Iowa fans. Then, Jim Bain came walking by and saw us sitting there reading the letters ... Kenny and I just kind of smirked. I don't think Bain was all that happy to see us. Kenny and I got a good laugh out of it later."

Arnold was drafted in the 5th round of the 1982 NBA draft by the Dallas Mavericks. He didn't make the team, but continued to work out, trying to catch on with a pro team for a couple of years.

Then, the summer of 1984 came along and everything changed. Arnold and Henry were 25 years old.

"Kenny was still working out," said Henry. "I was back in Elgin getting ready to start work as a teacher's assistant. Kenny called me and said he had passed out after working out in Ames. But he kind of blew past it, saying it was really hot that day and he hadn't eaten anything. He was not the type of guy who wanted you to worry."

A month later, Arnold called Henry again. "Kenny said that he passed out again," said Henry. "I told him to get to a doctor *now*. He came back home to Chicago and the doctors he saw didn't find anything. So, I told him to go to Iowa City, where he reached out to John Streif, who helped Kenny get an appointment at the University of Iowa Hospital. That's when the doctors there found the tumor in his brain."

Henry said they were all in shock at the diagnosis. "Nobody ever dreamed of him having a brain tumor," said Henry. "But the first thing that Kenny said was, 'Mike, I'm beating this.'"

Arnold underwent surgery in early October. "I took his mom from Chicago to Iowa City for the surgery," said Henry. "I had to get back to Elgin for work, so I would leave Iowa City at 3 a.m., drive to Elgin, get done with work at 2:30 p.m. and drive back to Iowa City. I did that about every other day for three weeks … and stayed in Iowa City on weekends."

Henry's sister Nannette was in school at Iowa at the time. "Nannette spent many of those nights at the hospital with Kenny to make sure he was OK," said Henry. "When you're in that situation, you really don't think a lot about it, you just do what you can to try to help."

Nannette Henry Combs was 20 years old at the time but stayed with Arnold in the hospital as often as she could. "We just tried to make sure that someone was with him as much as possible," she said. "I told the staff to call me if he's not sleeping or not having a good night. Sometimes, it was just a matter of sitting with him and talking or holding his hand. Or just being there, so he could be as comfortable as possible and to let him know 'You're not alone.'"

After the surgery, Arnold was able to keep his attitude – and everyone else's – as upbeat as possible. "It took Kenny a while to be able to do much of anything or say a whole lot,"

64

said Henry. "But he kept a 'What's next?' attitude and stayed positive. He was so positive that everyone around him stayed positive too. We all just felt like, 'What's it gonna take?'"

Arnold, Henry and those closest to them were prepared to do whatever would be necessary to keep moving forward.

The 1978-79 Iowa Hawkeyes tied for the Big Ten Conference championship. Front row: Greg Boyle, Dick Peth, Kirk Speraw, Ronnie Lester, Randy Norton, Tom Norman, Kenny Arnold. Back row: Vince Brookins, William Mayfield, Steve Waite, Mike Henry, Steve Krafcisin, Kevin Boyle. *(Photo courtesy of The University of Iowa.)*

The 1979-80 Iowa Hawkeyes overcame a great deal of adversity to earn a trip to the Final Four. Front row: Sandy Blom, Coach Ken Burmeister, Coach Jim Rosborough, Coach Lute Olson, Coach Tony McAndrews, Wade Jones. Second row: Kevin Boyle, Mark Gannon, Mike Henry, Steve Waite, Steve Krafcisin, Mike Heller, Vince Brookins. Third row: Randy Norton, Greg Boyle, Mike Arens, Jon Darsee, Bobby Hansen, Ronnie Lester, Kenny Arnold, Kirk Speraw, Tom Cummings. *(Photo courtesy of The University of Iowa.)*

Kenny Arnold drives to the basket for a layup against Ohio State in front of a sellout crowd at The Field House in Iowa City in 1982. Arnold's jersey in this photo is the inspiration for the "Teammates For Life" shirts created to honor the former Hawkeye great. Mark Gannon (#44) is seen in the background. Iowa defeated the Buckeyes, 76-66, in this game. *(Photo courtesy of The University of Iowa.)*

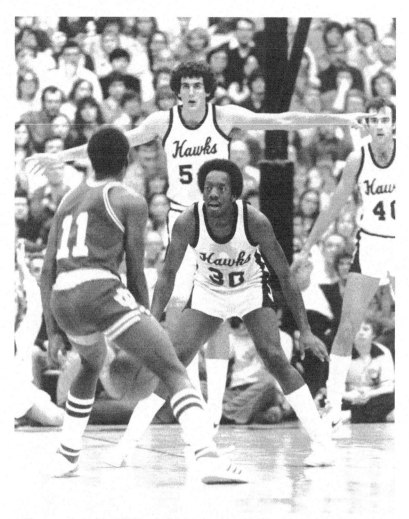

Kenny Arnold (#30) defends against Indiana's Isiah Thomas (#11) in a game at The Field House in 1981. Steve Krafcisin (#54) and Kevin Boyle (#40) are prepared to help. The Hawkeyes defeated the Hoosiers, 78-65, to complete a season sweep against Indiana, which went on to win the national title that season. *(Photo courtesy of The University of Iowa.)*

Kenny Arnold (#30) drives around an Ohio State defender in front of a packed house in Iowa City. The Iowa teams that Arnold played on were victorious in 85 percent of their games at The Field House, with a 46-8 record. *(Photo courtesy of The University of Iowa.)*

Kenny Arnold (#30) drives to the basket against Northern Iowa in December of 1979. Vince Brookins (#32) battles for the rebound while Ronnie Lester (#12) is in the background. Iowa defeated the Panthers, 78-46, in front of a packed crowd at The Field House in Iowa City. *(Photo courtesy of The University of Iowa.)*

Kenny Arnold, Mike "Tree" Henry, Steve Waite and Vince Brookins spent a great deal of time together off the court during their years at The University of Iowa.

Kenny Arnold and Mike "Tree" Henry sit together at the nursing home where Arnold resides. The two men, who were born on the same day in 1959, have been like brothers since their days of playing basketball for the Hawkeyes.

71

Matt Dunning (far left) and I traveled to Chicago in August of 2016 to help Kenny Arnold try out a speech-generating device from our company, Talk To Me Technologies. Ronnie Lester (front), Mike Arens (behind Lester) and Mike "Tree" Henry (back right) were there that day to support their friend and former teammate.

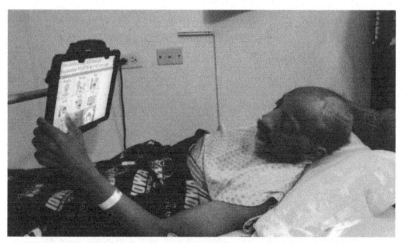

Kenny Arnold is able to communicate using his Zuvo 12 speech-generating device from Talk To Me Technologies. He is able to make choices on the touch screen to speak words and phrases. *(Photo courtesy of Mike Henry.)*

The University of Iowa men's basketball team honored Kenny Arnold on January 15, 2017 by wearing the "Teammates For Life" shirts during their warm-ups before a game at Northwestern University in Evanston, Illinois. *(Photo courtesy of Mike Henry.)*

In December of 2016, current Iowa basketball coach Fran McCaffery, his wife Margaret, former Iowa basketball coach Lute Olson and his wife Kelly hold up the shirts that honor Kenny Arnold and his "Teammates For Life." *(Photo courtesy of Mike Henry.)*

After an Iowa victory over Iowa State in December of 2016, Mike "Tree" Henry introduced my son Ben to former Iowa basketball coach Lute Olson. Coach Olson autographed a basketball for Ben and was as gracious with his time as always.

On February 18, 2017, there was a "White-Out" game at Carver-Hawkeye Arena to honor Kenny Arnold and his "Teammates For Life." My wife Emily and I took four of our children to this game and we had a great time.

Kenny Arnold was all smiles watching the "White-Out" game at Carver-Hawkeye Arena in February of 2017 with several of his friends at the nursing home where he resides.

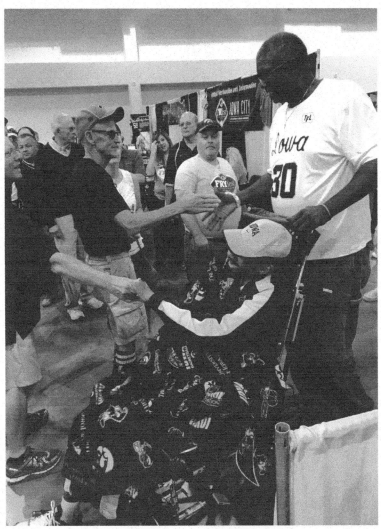

Kenny Arnold returned to Iowa City for Fry Fest in 2017. Fans lined up to shake hands, share stories and take photos with Arnold and Mike "Tree" Henry.

Vince Brookins, Ben Gallagher and Kenny Arnold pose for a photo together at Fry Fest in 2017. Fans were thrilled to get a chance to visit with Arnold and his former teammates at this event.

Mike "Tree" Henry and John Streif offer words of encouragement to Kenny Arnold as the golf cart he is riding in with Henry is about to enter Kinnick Stadium on September 2, 2017. The 1980 Iowa Hawkeye Final Four team was honored at halftime of the football game that day.

The Kinnick Stadium crowd erupted with an ovation to support Kenny Arnold and his "Teammates For Life" when Arnold's name was announced to the 68,000 Iowa fans in attendance on September 2, 2017. When Arnold raised his left arm to wave to the crowd, the noise was deafening. Shown in the north end zone are Vince Brookins, Mike "Tree" Henry, Kenny Arnold, Kirk Speraw, Marty Gallagher, Ben Gallagher, Jackie Reed, Bobby Hansen, Jon Darsee, Mike Arens, Greg Boyle, Coach Johnie Butler, Ronnie Lester, Kevin Boyle and Steve Waite.

My son Ben, Kenny Arnold and me. This photo was taken on Friday, September 1, 2017 after the Fry Fest activities.

Kenny Arnold and Mike "Tree" Henry share a fist bump as the two spend time together at the nursing home where Arnold resides.

Kenny Arnold, Ronnie Lester and Mike "Tree" Henry display the shirts that were designed to honor Arnold and his "Teammates For Life."

CHAPTER 5

Thirty Years Later...

"Never meet your heroes."

I don't know who came up with that phrase. But it wasn't a sports fan who grew up in Iowa in the early 1980s.

———————————

In the summer of 2016, before heading to bed one night, I read a story on a website called AllHawkeyes.com. The story, written by Pat Harty, was titled "The Courage and Grace of Kenny Arnold is Truly Inspiring."

It had been 30 years since I had first met Arnold at our high school athletic banquet that was so abruptly cut short because of my classmate's prank phone call. I had not followed the details of Arnold's situation since 1986.

My life had changed dramatically in the three decades that followed. In 2016, I was a husband to my wife Emily, a father to five wonderful children (Carly, Molly, Ben, Sophie and Leo) and the CEO/Co-Founder of a company – Talk To Me Technologies – that has a mission to give a voice to people who struggle to speak. We manufacture and sell speech-generating devices to people who cannot otherwise talk. We work with people of all ages who have diagnoses like autism, Down's syndrome, cerebral palsy, brain injuries, ALS and strokes.

From reading Harty's story that night, I learned that Arnold's life had changed dramatically, as well. But unlike me, many of his changes were not for the better.

At that point, according to Harty's story, Arnold was in a wheelchair and his physical limitations were many. The former star athlete needed help to get dressed, help to get to his appointments and daily assistance for things many of us take for granted. Harty had also written, "Arnold's ability to speak has been ravaged by his health issues." The person who was there by Arnold's side through it all, providing the necessary assistance, was Henry.

At that time, I was almost 47 years old. It had been 36 years since I had pretended to be the 1980 Hawkeyes on my driveway. But when I went to bed that night after reading Harty's story, I felt that there might be something that our company could do to help.

So, I got out of bed, went back downstairs to my office and sent an email to Harty, explaining that I was a big fan of the 1980 Hawkeyes as a boy … and that Talk To Me Technologies is a company that provides speech-generating devices to people who have difficulty speaking. I wrote that I just wanted to check in and see if there was anything that our company could do to help Arnold.

At 11:52 p.m. that night, I sent that email to Pat Harty.

The next day, Harty replied that he would forward my contact information to "Tree" Henry and Mark Gannon, two of Arnold's teammates who Harty had interviewed for his story.

Gannon called me and shared the details. The situation sounded bleak. Gannon told me that Arnold had always been a positive and upbeat person – despite his health issues – but that recently, he had taken a bit of a turn. Hospice was a consideration, said Gannon. But he could see the potential that a speech-generating device might bring to the situation.

Gannon asked me if Talk To Me Technologies had any reps working in the Chicago area. We didn't. However, I told him that I would like to see Arnold myself – if possible – and bring along the top person in our company (and the industry, in my opinion) at helping to evaluate individuals and make a recommendation for what might be the most helpful.

Gannon said that would be great. That conversation took place on Thursday, August 18. Matt Dunning and I arrived in Chicago on Monday, August 22, four days later.

———————

Dunning and I had started Talk To Me Technologies with my sister Katie back in 2006. Dunning is a Speech-Language Pathologist and a technology expert. He was the perfect person to assess if there was something we could provide to help Arnold communicate.

Arnold had been living in a nursing home on the South Side of Chicago since 2010. His insurance situation was not the greatest and there wasn't much available in order to fund a device for him. But as a company, Talk To Me Technologies was celebrating our 10th anniversary that month, so we had picked a few ways that we could donate our time and resources as a sign of gratitude.

Arnold was an easy choice. We had decided to donate a new device to him, if we could provide something that would help.

When Dunning and I arrived at the nursing home, we were greeted immediately by three of Arnold's teammates at Iowa – "Tree" Henry, Ronnie Lester and Mike Arens – along with Jackie Reed, a close friend of the former Hawkeye basketball players. All four of these guys are Chicago natives, although Lester and Arens were both living in Florida, but happened to be back "home" in Chicago at that time.

Dunning and I had prepared a demonstration device – a Zuvo 12 – for Arnold. This device has a 12-inch screen and would enable Arnold to make choices on the touch screen to speak words and phrases associated with things like pain, positioning and general help. For example, Arnold would be able to press an image on the screen to say, "I am in pain" and it would open a page that would show body parts, and a pain scale of one to five, for him to further elaborate. He could also press images on the screen to say things like, "I am short of breath," "I need to be turned," "I am hungry," "I am thirsty," "I am hot," "I am cold," and "Please turn on the TV." Things that a person would want or need to say to a caregiver.

There was also a special "Kenny" page that included phrases like, "My name is Kenny Arnold," "I played basketball for the Iowa Hawkeyes," "We made it to the Final Four in 1980" and "My teammates at Iowa are still my good friends today. We are teammates for life!" And we added an icon that opened up a page with a photo of the 1980 Hawkeye basketball team.

The vocabulary options on these devices are limitless. The number of options on a page can be increased, the number of words can be expanded, a keyboard can be added to enable a user to create his or her own messages … the opportunities are bound only by the needs and wants of the person using the device. And the options can be easily edited as those needs and wants change.

In this case, Dunning and I attached the Zuvo 12 device to a mount that had four wheels, so it could be rolled up to Arnold, whether he was sitting in his chair or lying down on his bed. It could also be easily detached so that it could rest in his lap, if he chose to do that.

We were hopeful that this would be a good option for him.

When Arnold was wheeled into the meeting room to see us, though, he looked very tired. He was slumped in his wheelchair, his yellow Iowa baseball cap was pulled down almost over his eyes and his body appeared frail. While Arnold was only 57 years old at the time, he appeared to be 25 years older.

However, the moment that he saw his friends in the room, a smile emerged on his face. You could see that he was happy, but there was something wrong. He was in pain. Arnold was suffering from a great deal of pain in his right hip and it had become extremely difficult for him to sit up for very long.

Dunning worked with Arnold from a clinical standpoint with the demonstration device. He determined, for example, that Arnold had a vision deficit on his right side (possibly a side effect of one of his strokes) that would need to be addressed by how the images on the screen were organized to help him compensate. He also determined that a T-handled stylus would help Arnold accurately press the screen where he intended.

Meanwhile, I was talking to Arnold and asking him questions, waiting for his responses with the device. In addition, I had brought my 1986 Starmont High School yearbook and showed him two photos from the night he spoke at our athletic banquet, prior to the police entering the building and the evacuation. Arnold looked at me with his best "what in the heck happened" expression. I explained the prank phone call story and how he was a victim of his own fame and popularity … and he and his teammates laughed.

While Dunning and I were working with Arnold, I noticed a tear roll down the right side of his face. It was apparent that he was uncomfortable. Dunning asked Arnold if he was ready to take a break from the technology and Arnold nodded. It was time to end our session. Arnold smiled and wanted everyone to meet him up in his room in 15 minutes. The caregiver then wheeled him out of the meeting room.

Henry was optimistic. "You can see he can do it," he said. "This could really be motivating for him."

Then, Henry shared with the group of us a story about how recently, Arnold was tugging at his sweatshirt and trying to say something to his caregiver. All that he could say, though, was a "huh" sound, which he repeated over and over. The caregiver feared it was Arnold's heart, so she wanted to get a nurse … but in reality, Arnold was just trying to say that he was "hot" and wanted to take off his sweatshirt.

"These are the kinds of things that keep happening," said Henry. "People see Kenny in his wheelchair and they think he doesn't know what's going on, but he's sharp as a tack. It's just so frustrating for him to have to keep waiting for people to guess what he's saying … or what he wants."

Then Henry talked about the immense pain that Arnold was suffering in his right hip. "Did you see that tear roll down his cheek?" he asked. "That's from the pain he's in all the time. He's the toughest person I've ever met, but that constant pain is just awful."

Lester thanked Dunning and me for making the trip and expressed hope that this type of device might provide some clear benefits for Arnold.

When Arnold was back in his room, we went up to see him again. Arnold was in his bed but sitting up a bit as the head of his bed was elevated to a 45-degree angle. He was wearing a black Iowa polo shirt and covered in a black-and-gold Iowa basketball blanket.

Henry asked Arnold what he thought of the device and Arnold smiled and nodded. We placed the Zuvo 12 on Arnold's lap and he immediately pressed the icon to get to the 1980 Iowa team photo. Then his smile almost doubled in size. He stared at that photo and grinned, clearly very proud. His entire demeanor had changed from when he was first wheeled into the meeting room downstairs.

As the memories of that team were being tossed back and forth, someone asked if there was anyone besides Arnold and Kevin Boyle in the Hawkeye senior class of 1982. Lester, who was drafted in 1980, and Henry, who completed his eligibility in 1981, weren't sure.

Arnold had the answer, though. He found the team photo on his device and pointed with his left hand at the player in the back row, uniform number 20.

"That's right," said Henry. "Darsee!"

Jon Darsee was a senior on the Iowa basketball team in 1982 with Kevin Boyle and Kenny Arnold. The one person in the room who knew that was Arnold … and now he was able to share it.

Before Dunning and I left Arnold's room that afternoon, I reached out to shake Arnold's left hand. He grabbed my hand, squeezed it tightly and held onto it. The look on Arnold's face as he pursed his lips and nodded told me all that I needed to know.

It's rare that you get the opportunity, as an adult, to help someone who you pretended to be as a 10-year-old kid. But this was that moment. I hoped that we were doing something that would make a difference for him.

As we left the facility, Dunning and I exchanged good-byes with Henry, Lester, Arens and Reed. Then we headed out the door. We took the demonstration device back with us but planned to ship a new device to Arnold within a week.

On our five-hour drive back to Cedar Falls, Dunning and I discussed Arnold's situation and how successful he might be with his new device. We both felt that he could use it effectively, but he would need the support staff at the nursing home to be on board and encourage him to use it. People would need to be patient enough for Arnold to become more accurate with his selections. And Arnold would have to want to use it.

We were cautiously optimistic. But also aware of Arnold's poor health and the amount of pain he was suffering.

Through the first 10 years in this business of helping people who were unable to speak, and meeting some of the strongest and most inspirational people you could ever imagine, I was certain that I had never met anyone tougher or more inspiring than Kenny Arnold.

CHAPTER 6

"Kenny's Back!"

Within a week after Matt Dunning and I had returned from seeing Arnold in Chicago, our company shipped a new Zuvo 12 device to him that was set up specifically for his communication needs. Henry delivered it to Arnold at the nursing home and the two of them began practicing with it immediately.

I hoped that it would be of some help to Arnold. I felt that if we could make his life a little better – even in a small way – it would've been a success.

I was thrilled with the feedback from Henry within a few days.

Henry called me on Wednesday, August 31, 2016 in the late afternoon. "Kenny hasn't stopped smiling for three hours," he said. "He's so excited about his device! The nurses here are losing their minds. He's smiling and focused ... his whole attitude has changed. This gives him something to focus on, instead of the pain."

Henry couldn't help from becoming emotional as he continued. "Kenny's back!" he said. "He was really down in the dumps before you guys came. He was close to giving up, but this has completely turned him around mentally. He's back to being the Kenny that we all know and love.

"Kenny saw the device as a lifeline," Henry said. "He really perked up after receiving it. We're very grateful."

That was music to my ears. It's difficult to explain the pride you have in helping someone who was a childhood hero.

———————————

The next day, on Thursday, September 1, Henry called me again.

"Kenny is so positive now," he said. "He's maneuvering so much better on the device. He's really excited and never stops playing around with it. The nurses are getting into it. Kenny is so laser-focused and competitive ... he's so happy."

Henry talked about how Arnold seemed to have turned a corner in the last few days. "He's in absolute heaven," he said. "His attitude change has been amazing. The last few months, Kenny had really been depressed. But this device is giving him something to think about. A week ago, he needed to be turned in his bed once every 15 minutes because of the pain in his hip, but today, he only needed to be turned once in three hours."

The outlook had changed dramatically and not just for Arnold. Henry talked about how recently, it had been difficult when it came time to leave Arnold because of the fear of what might happen before he could return. "Now, when I leave, I can tell him, 'I KNOW I'm going to see you again!'" said Henry. "He's so light-hearted again, this is the *real* Kenny."

Henry and I discussed creating a Facebook page for Arnold that would enable Hawkeye fans to post messages of encouragement – and share memories – with Arnold. A couple of days later, on September 3, Henry and his sister Nannette Henry Combs had created the page. And the result was immediate and overwhelming, as Iowa fans from all over the globe were posting messages and photos, sharing their words of encouragement with Arnold.

And it wasn't just Hawkeye fans who were posting messages for Arnold to see. In the first few days, Arnold's new Facebook page was drawing memories, words of encouragement and old photos from former Iowa teammates, college friends, parents of former Hawkeye players, former Iowa staff members and former opponents from Iowa State, Indiana and Purdue, among others.

Here is a sampling of the initial messages that arrived for Arnold:

"So many thinking of you Kenny and you'll always be loved in the state of Iowa."

"Hey Kenny … Favorite moments hanging out in your room at Hillcrest with Tree and talking about anything … and definitely when you and Tree took me to Chicago and we stayed at Tree's house … First time eating gumbo and learning the ropes … Kenny, you're the best."

"What's up Kenny! I was a junior at Providence Catholic high school the year you made it to the Final Four! You inspired so many ballplayers, especially me, to dream about playing in the most important games in college sports. You represented your culture and Iowa with class! I am proud to have had the opportunity to meet you. My thoughts and prayers are with you Bruh!"

"It was a privilege to watch you play but it was more important to watch you grow and mature as a man … You were always humble, a team player and a kind young man."

"Huge Hawkeye fan all my life and attended UI after high school. Idolized Ronnie Lester growing up but it was Kenny Arnold I emulated by wearing the same high top Converse shoes he used to wear. Kenny never got enough credit for saving our season when Lester went down to injury."

"Hi Kenny – thoughts and prayers go out to you from Des Moines! We're all Hawkeyes for Life!"

"This was a super team that always gave us nightmares! One of the best I ever played against!"

"Kenny Arnold what can I say; you are a pure inspiration of courage and strength in the face of adversity and a fighter at heart filled with love. Peace my brother and thank you for just being you."

"Kenny Arnold, you helped put Iowa BB on the map. Plus it's always fun to watch champions."

"Kenny you are one of my all time favorite Hawkeyes but also one of my all time favorite people. Can't tell you how much I admire you. Iowa Basketball is lucky to have had you play for them. The love of your teammates and coaches is a true measure of how much you mean to us all. Love you my friend. It's Great to be a Hawkeye. You were one of the GREATS."

"Hi Kenny! I grew up watching your Hawkeye teams! All the best to you!"

"I remember being in the Fieldhouse when the Hawks came home after beating Georgetown to get to the Final Four. What a great team and Kenny was a huge part of it."

And on and on it went. Messages pouring in to share memories and well wishes with Arnold from people he never met … and friends he had not heard from in decades.

Kenny loved hearing from his friends and Hawkeye fans. But the pain in his hip was not going away. The prevailing thought was that physical therapy might be the best thing for Arnold's pain, but there were no funds available to pay for this. Henry decided to set up a "Go Fund Me" page for Arnold and we could use the Facebook page, which continued to add friends all the time, to promote this.

Meanwhile, throughout September, Henry and I continued to discuss Arnold's progress. Text messages from Henry detailed Arnold's success with the Zuvo 12 speech device and his joy about all the messages he was receiving.

On September 8, Henry texted, "Thanks so much Marty from Kenny and I. Kenny has a big smile on his face and is very happy. I'm still with him and he hasn't stopped smiling since I got here and all the nurses have been stopping in to see the device and are thrilled for him. Wishing all the patients had them."

On September 16, Henry texted, "The nurses had taken the device down for some reason but I set it back up as soon as I got there and KA was happy and jumped right on it. … It is great to see him so focused and even with the pain, he just kept working with no complaints. Huge improvement attitude wise."

––––––––––––

Late in the afternoon of September 20, 2016, Arnold is in the lunchroom at his nursing home in Chicago. One nurse begins to push him back to his room in his wheelchair, while another nurse and Tree Henry follow along. The trip is short, but when they arrive in Arnold's room, he is wincing and cringing, feeling a lot of pain.

After he sits in the same position for very long, Arnold's hip begins to hurt. His left hand is in a fist and he presses his left arm against the arm of his wheelchair in an effort to reposition himself to ease the pain and discomfort.

The two nurses lift Arnold up out of his chair and get him into his bed.

"Are you comfortable now?" asks Henry, who knows that his friend doesn't want to ask for help.

Arnold nods but his lips are pursed and his teeth are clenched. He looks to his left, across the room to his Zuvo 12 speech device attached to the mount sitting against the wall. Arnold points to the device with his left hand.

"Got it," says Henry, who rolls the device over to Arnold's bed so he can use it.

Arnold lifts his left hand, presses an image on the screen, then another … and the team photo of the 1980 Iowa Hawkeye basketball team appears on the device. His body begins to relax and the pained expression on his face is gone.

"There's your guys," says Henry.

Arnold looks at Henry and smiles. Henry smiles back and they share a quiet laugh.

On September 21, Henry texted, "Cool note. We had to wait quite a while for the nurses to get him back in bed and he was really hurting bad. But as soon as he got in bed, he motioned for me to get the device and he started punching buttons and had a big smile. It immediately calmed him down. It is amazing to see the effect it has. He is in such a peaceful state with it. He was fighting back tears from the pain and went from that to a smile and relaxed body in about a minute.

Thanks again. I know that has to inspire you to keep doing what you do and please know how much it is appreciated!

"Just taking care of my brother and it is so awesome to see the response to Kenny and all the good that has come from Pat's article and what you did. So many people have written posts or sent messages and that means so much to Kenny and all of us who love him but I truly believe the people who are seeing what we are doing will be inspired. I have several messages from people who feel a sense of hope from seeing the technology is there to maybe help them with their own situations which is priceless.

"This gets better and better with the possibilities the device opens up for him. ... We all just do what we need to do for him and don't really think about it but when you do stop and take it all in and see the effect the story and Kenny have on people, it is very cool. That is why we are trying to share it as much as possible so it may inspire others to keep fighting or for those who can to help others.'"

In mid-September, Henry posted a video of Arnold touching an image on his device, which generated the following message: "Thanks fans and friends."

Beneath the video, Henry wrote the following message: "I had the pleasure of doing a radio interview this morning on KCJJ of Iowa City with Pat Harty and Marty Gallagher about Kenny Arnold and his progress with the tablet from Talk To Me Technologies. It was fun talking with these gentlemen and then I went to visit KA. I read him the names of all of his new Facebook friends and all of the posts (I was there a while :-)) and he really enjoyed that. I can not express how much of a difference that makes for him. He was having a rough day pain wise from his hip but he worked on his tablet and listened to the names and stories and kept a smile on his face as he remembered many of the names and stories. Please continue to check in on Kenny's page from time to time and please share it with others. Thanks again to everyone and Kenny sends his thanks as well!!!"

Receiving this feedback from Henry and watching the messages pour in through Arnold's Facebook page was incredibly inspiring. The question that kept rising up was "What else can we do to help?"

My son Ben was 13 years old at the time. He was in 8th grade at Storm Lake Middle School and an avid Hawkeye fan. Ben enjoys watching baseball and football, but basketball is his favorite, both to play and to watch. Ben and I love watching games on TV together and try to go to at least one game in Iowa City each season. Ben was very interested in Arnold's progress and the entire story about how his Hawkeye teammates had stuck together to help him. Sharing everything that Henry was doing – and the personal sacrifices Henry was making for his friend – was an excellent life lesson and example for Ben to see, as well.

As Ben and I were shooting baskets on our driveway together one day in late September, we came up with the idea of creating a "Kenny Arnold Facebook Challenge." We decided to challenge people to post a message or video (tagging Kenny Arnold) that shared a favorite Hawkeye memory, a message for Kenny Arnold and then tag three friends to do the same.

We posted a video of Ben, saying, "Hi, this is Ben Gallagher and I'm doing the Kenny Arnold Facebook Challenge. My favorite Hawkeye memory was when Adam Woodbury had the game-winning tip-in at the buzzer against Temple in the NCAA Tournament last year. My message to Kenny is that we think about you a lot and we hope you're doing well." Then Ben mentioned three people he wanted to tag to challenge them to do the same.

I posted a video with a message, as well. So did Henry. And that started another run of messages, videos and stream of memories that could boost Arnold's spirits.

Henry called me a few days later. "This is absolutely amazing," he said. "I'm so emotional with all the responses from people we haven't heard from in years. I showed Kenny all the videos and he lit up. He grinned when he saw Ben's video. He's calm now, not uptight like before. You can see the relaxation.

"If Kenny died tomorrow, he would be one happy man. We were losing him before, now he's back to himself. He's back to trying again. Kenny's back!"

A few days later, Henry texted me, "Kenny loved the Challenge. I showed him all the videos and posts. ... He is so grateful for all the attention. You should start seeing videos from the players tonight which could get a little crazy.

"Many people are responding and we have connected with several friends we haven't talked to in years all because of Kenny. Thanks so much for starting this. You have literally changed his world and mine as his friend and helper and touched so many people which is what we have always wanted to do.

"I will be talking to a friend tonight who was like a little sister (and of course Kenny's too) my senior year at Iowa. She was about 9 years old then and I lived with her family for a couple of years as they kind of adopted me and we became family. We had lost touch over the years but she saw the Challenge last night and I'Md me and we went back and forth for 5 hours until 4 this morning and plan on talking on the phone tonight for the first time in probably 25 years. That means the world to me as I get my little sister back and it's all because of this. I have been in tears of joy for the last 24 hours over this and a couple of other people who reached out. This is so much bigger than it even started out to be and I can't thank you enough my friend."

My wife Emily and I were out for a walk that evening when I received that text from Henry. I remember I had to stop walking to read it and the goosebumps were immediate.

But the question remained, "What else can we do to help?" We didn't realize that our best idea was already in the works.

CHAPTER 7

The Shirts

In August of 2016, after I returned home from visiting Arnold in his Chicago nursing home and having him try out a speech device, my son Ben and I had a conversation. We talked about all the things that Arnold's teammates have been doing for him through the years. Ben thought it would be a fun idea to do something to honor Arnold and his teammates who I had met up to this point.

When Henry told us in early September that we were a part of this special group, Arnold's "Teammates For Life," it felt like a tremendous compliment for Ben and me. After kicking around ideas for a couple of weeks, Ben decided to create a shirt that would make use of that phrase that the 1980 Hawkeye team had used many times to describe their togetherness.

Ben has always had an eye for design and had long been interested in what looks good and what's in style. For example, Ben – and all his buddies, it seems – are very much into what shoes each NBA or college basketball player wears … and in fact, I think Ben could tell me, within two minutes, what type of shoe each basketball player is wearing in any given game that we are watching.

So, Ben went to work designing a "Teammates For Life" logo. He created a logo that had bold TFL letters inside an outline of the state of Iowa. Then, he looked at the basketball uniforms the Hawkeyes used to wear in the years that Arnold was playing.

Ben came up with an idea that I thought looked great … and made perfect sense to honor Arnold.

The shirt was white with a black "Iowa" script on the front, outlined in yellow, reminiscent of the Hawkeye uniforms of the early 1980s. There was a black number "30" on the front (Arnold's jersey number) and a "TFL" logo in the upper-left corner above the Iowa script. On the back of the long-sleeve shirt was another number 30, along with the last name of the person for whom we would order the shirt.

I was proud of Ben and happy to order a dozen shirts. We would order seven shirts for our family, one for Matt Dunning, and one each for Arnold, Henry, Lester and Gannon.

The shirts were completed by the middle of October and I shipped them out to the guys.

———————————

One afternoon in late October of 2016, Henry walks into Arnold's room at the nursing home, carrying a bag in his right hand. Arnold is laying in bed, covered up in his black-and-gold Hawkeye blanket.

"Hey, I got a surprise for you," says Henry.

Henry reaches into the bag and pulls out a TFL shirt and holds it up, first showing Arnold the front of the shirt ... and then the back. Arnold's eyes get wide and his mouth hangs open. He appears shocked but happy.

"Ben did this for you ... just to show you how much everyone thinks of you," Henry tells his friend.

Arnold starts shaking his head side-to-side in disbelief.

"This one's for you and he also made one for me," says Henry, pulling out another shirt from the bag.

Then Henry lays Arnold's shirt across his friend's chest. Arnold puts his left hand across the shirt and starts rubbing it. Arnold looks over at Henry and his eyes start to well up with tears ... and then Henry starts to cry himself. Tears of joy.

———————

I sent Henry a few photos of Emily, our kids and me wearing our shirts and asked him to share those with Arnold. In the meantime, Henry had a few photos taken of Arnold holding his shirt ... and Henry, Lester and Arnold together holding a couple of the shirts, so you could see both the front and back.

Then, Henry posted a few of the photos on Arnold's Facebook page. Things took off from there. "At first, I thought the shirts were really cool," said Henry. "Then, I posted the pictures on Facebook as a shout out to Ben. On my one-hour drive home, everything changed. I got about 100 messages … people were asking 'Where can I get this shirt?' In that moment, it went from the coolest shirt to something REALLY special."

Henry called me on the phone that evening and he was excited. He told me how his phone was blowing up from people asking how they could obtain a shirt like that.

"Vince Brookins and I had been talking, asking ourselves, 'What can we do to help?'" said Henry. "My immediate response to the shirts – after getting that feedback from people – was 'this could be it.' We had been trying to think of something to raise funds and attention for Kenny. The shirts turned out to be the perfect idea."

Henry asked me to call Brookins, another member of the 1980 Final Four team, because Brookins would be the person to handle the financial decisions with the money we raised for the Kenny Arnold Fund.

Brookins was a six-foot-five small forward for the Hawkeyes with a smooth outside jump shot that was often imitated by kids in Iowa in the early 1980s. He had quite a back story of his own.

Brookins had broken both of his legs as a third-grader and was in traction for an extended period. Then as a sophomore at Collinwood High School in Cleveland, Ohio, he was stabbed in the chest in a race riot. "It punctured my heart," said Brookins. "I have a scar from the center of my chest up under my ribs to the center of my back."

Most Hawkeye fans will recall that Brookins shot the ball extremely well during the team's NCAA Tournament run to the Final Four in 1980. A junior at the time, Brookins scored 17 points against North Carolina State, 21 points versus Syracuse and 22 points in the Regional Final against Georgetown. During that three-game stretch, Brookins made 22 of 34 shots from the floor (65 percent) and 16 of 19 free throws (84 percent).

"I was just waiting for an opportunity to help carry the load," said Brookins. "I wanted to show that I could play. In practice, I'd been trying to prepare for the opportunity. I had gotten to a place where I was not going to worry about making mistakes … and I got locked in."

During our initial discussion, Brookins and I talked about the TFL shirts and the potential for possibly having a "White Out" game sometime this season at Carver-Hawkeye Arena. It might have been a little far-fetched to consider that as a possibility, but it seemed that the stars were aligning.

Within a couple of days, Henry, Brookins and I had a conference call and decided to begin selling the new TFL shirts online for $30 apiece, a nice round number that was also Arnold's jersey number. Brookins found a vendor that would print up the shirts for us. The vendor also provided a web page for fans to see the shirts and place their orders.

The TFL shirts were officially for sale. All the proceeds would go to the Kenny Arnold Fund, which Henry had established to help take care of Arnold's medical needs that he could not afford, mainly the physical therapy treatments.

Fans and friends of Arnold began ordering their shirts and posting photos of themselves wearing the shirts on Arnold's Facebook page.

At some point that fall, both Gannon and Henry told me that Coach Olson was returning to Iowa City for a basketball game against Iowa State on Thursday, December 8. Several of Coach Olson's former players were planning to attend the game, then get together afterward with Coach Olson at a gathering in Iowa City. Gannon and Henry extended an invitation to me to join them that night at the game and post-game gathering, and they said it would be great if Emily and Ben could attend too.

We were thrilled with that opportunity.

Before the game, we met Gannon, Henry and Henry's sister Nannette at a restaurant for a bite to eat. It was fun to catch up with them. The TFL shirts were just starting to sell online and people were posting photos of themselves wearing the shirts on Arnold's Facebook page.

When we arrived at Carver-Hawkeye Arena, we headed down to our seats, which were outstanding, just a few rows up from the court. The first person who met us was John Streif, the legendary former trainer at Iowa, who gave us each a warm welcome. He handed to me a copy of that day's Cedar Rapids Gazette sports page, which included a story by Mike Hlas (one of my favorite sportswriters in Iowa) about Arnold's story.

We were sitting among several former Hawkeye players, people who were the TV stars of my youth. I sat between Ben and Emily. To Ben's left was Jon Darsee and to Emily's right was Michael Payne. Directly in front of us were people like Todd Berkenpas, Kevin Boyle, Greg Stokes and Henry. At halftime, Ronnie Lester made his way over from across the arena where he was sitting to greet us and thank us for coming.

It was a truly remarkable and memorable night.

At the time, Iowa started three freshmen in their lineup and only one senior, Peter Jok. The Hawks were only 4-5 at the time, with a young team trying to find its way. The in-state rival Cyclones, on the other hand, were 6-2 and had been ranked in the nation's Top 25 since the beginning of the previous season. Iowa State was led by three players who would eventually play in the NBA: Monte Morris, Deonte Burton and Naz Mitrou-Long. On paper, this was a mismatch.

But like so many other things in life, the results aren't decided simply by what is most likely to happen. There are so many other factors at play, including effort, intelligence, grit, determination, confidence and resilience. These are all traits that Arnold and his former teammates know well. With Coach Olson in attendance at the arena that his program built, it was wonderful to watch Coach Fran McCaffery's young team battle to a 78-64 victory.

After the game, Emily, Ben and I visited with several of the former players down on the floor close to the hallway to the locker room. Henry was quick to introduce Ben to everyone, saying "This is Ben Gallagher ... He's the one who designed the shirts for Kenny!" And people immediately knew what Henry was talking about.

Coach McCaffery's wife, Margaret, actually sought Ben out and asked him if he would like to see the locker room and meet Coach Olson, who was visiting with some old friends. Ben was very excited. Margaret McCaffery led us to the locker room, where Henry introduced us to Coach Olson, who signed a basketball for Ben. "Coach, this is Ben Gallagher," said Henry. "He's the boy who designed the shirts for Kenny." To my surprise, Coach Olson knew about the shirts and the fund-raising efforts.

I was not aware at the time, but the night before this game, Coach Olson and some of his former players got together at Coach McCaffery's house. Henry had brought shirts for both coaches and he took a photo of Coach Olson, his wife Kelly, and Coach McCaffery and his wife Margaret, holding up a couple of the shirts.

"They were very proud," said Henry. "Lute cares tremendously about Kenny. Fran heard the story and it hit home with him because of everything his son Patrick has been through with cancer. Plus, Fran is the same age as the guys from our team and Lute was always a coach he looked up to. Fran has been very supportive and hasn't hesitated at all about anything we've asked. He's been there 100 percent."

It had been 35 years since I had last seen Coach Olson at the Maryville Café across the street from my high school, but he looked almost exactly the same. And he was just as nice to us on this night as he was back then.

Margaret McCaffery also led us to the team's meeting room where Coach McCaffery was on a phone, giving his postgame commentary to a reporter. The look on Ben's face as we got the tour was priceless ... like a kid on Christmas morning, multiplied by 100.

Several of the current and former Iowa players signed autographs and took photos with Ben as we made our way back out to the floor. Henry told us that everyone would be meeting for a postgame celebration at the Vesta Restaurant, we told him we would see him there and we left.

I had taken Ben to Carver-Hawkeye Arena for games in previous seasons and we always had a terrific time, but nothing could compare to the "red carpet" treatment we received that night.

———————————

Emily, Ben and I walked into Vesta and were immediately greeted by Streif, who had nothing but extremely kind things to say. We talked to Streif about Arnold's current situation and how we hoped to continue fundraising efforts so that he could receive regular physical therapy.

Henry then brought Coach McCaffery over to meet us. He couldn't have been nicer to us and of course, after the big victory, he was in a great mood. Coach McCaffery signed Ben's basketball and thanked Ben for designing the shirts. He asked Ben what grade he was in, if he played basketball, what he thought of the game tonight and made Ben feel like a million bucks. We visited with the coach for about 10 minutes before he got pulled another direction. "I'll be coming back for you someday," Coach McCaffery told Ben, as he patted him on the back.

Henry continued introducing us to former Hawkeyes, who played for Coach Olson at Iowa. Each person was extremely kind, affable, self-deprecating and happy to visit with us. And every single person made Ben feel like he was the most important individual in the room. It was amazing.

One of the things the former Hawks from that era like to discuss is how Coach Olson only recruited people who would fit in well with his team. He didn't just want good *players*, he wanted good *people*. This is something that was stressed and in fact, multiple former Iowa basketball players told me that if a recruit came in to Iowa City for a visit back then, the current players would be able to vote later whether they would want that player to be a part of their team or not. If they voted with a "thumbs down," then Coach Olson would move on from that recruit. In theory, it sounds simple, but when your profession is based on wins and losses, it takes some guts – and confidence in your coaching abilities – to put that into practice.

The end result was not just that Coach Olson's teams had great chemistry and the whole was greater than the sum of its parts. The ultimate end result was that these young men were learning how to behave, handle adversity, display character and represent their families, communities and the university with grace and class.

"Start with good people and they'll find a way to be successful," Coach Olson told me as we talked about Kenny Arnold and how his teammates have looked out for him all these years. "We looked at our team as a family. We were TRULY a family. It's a family environment ... and if someone has problems, you help take care of him."

Teammates for life, without a doubt. It would be extremely difficult – if not impossible – to have a group of people so dedicated to helping each other and sticking together, if not for Coach Olson's resolve to build a team of people with high character.

It was obvious that evening as we met these individuals, one after the other – people like Lester, Waite, Hansen, Payne, King, Gannon, Mike Gatens and others – who were so gracious and generous with their time. It should make Hawkeye fans proud to know the quality of people associated with the Iowa basketball program and how genuinely they care about each other. It is obvious that it is a family-oriented program – including everyone we've met from Coach Olson and his players from the 1970s and 1980s through Coach McCaffery and his players of today.

At the end of the night, the former Hawks presented Ben with a TFL shirt that they had each autographed for him. Ben was smiling from ear to ear. "That was really nice of them to go out of their way to surprise me with that autographed shirt, but that's the kind of people they are," he said. When we headed home the next morning, Ben was still on cloud nine.

As this entire story about Arnold was developing, Facebook attention was growing and the shirts began to sell, Henry and I had received a handful of requests from various media outlets. We were more than happy to oblige, of course, whether it was a newspaper article, radio interview or podcast. The publicity would be a benefit for Arnold in one way or another.

One of the most memorable stories was written by John Keilman of The Chicago Tribune. The headline was "Lifetime teammates fight for Hawkeye legend" and the story ran in the December 18, 2016 edition of the newspaper.

The final paragraph in Keilman's story is a quote from Henry:

"We've all been part of something very, very special," Henry said. "I'm literally thankful every day for that. Just time with my buddy here is really important. He never gets down, never complains. The guys will tell you that when we visit, we come to cheer up Kenny. But we're the ones who come out cheered up."

The popularity of the TFL shirts continued to grow through the winter. On January 15, 2017, the Iowa basketball team wore the shirts during their warm-ups before a game at Northwestern University in Evanston, Illinois. Evanston is a suburb of Chicago, so it was a wonderful tribute to Arnold in the Big Ten arena closest to his home.

Midway through the second half of the game, the TV announcers talked about Kenny Arnold, his health issues and showed video clips of the Iowa team wearing the shirts in warm-ups before the game to honor Arnold.

This was an excellent gesture by Coach McCaffery and the Hawks. And the response on social media was tremendous.

The next day, Henry posted a photo on Facebook of Arnold and Henry sitting together at the nursing home, with big smiles on their faces. Along with the photo, Henry posted the following: "Just finishing up a visit with Kenny Arnold and had the honor to show him the pictures of the Hawks wearing his shirt in warmups at Northwestern and all of the great comments, pictures and videos everyone has posted. He is absolutely blown away from all of the love and support shown by the best fans and friends anywhere. His response was simply WOW!!! He sends his love and thanks to all. We shared many smiles, hugs and tears of joy and appreciation and I want to add my own thanks to everyone for your caring about my friend."

CHAPTER 8

The White Out

In late October of 2016, Henry, Brookins and I had our first discussion about the possibility of a "White Out" game at Carver-Hawkeye Arena as a tribute, and potential fundraiser, for Arnold. We envisioned a packed arena with fans wearing the TFL shirts to honor the former Iowa guard.

After studying the Hawkeye basketball schedule, the only date that would provide an opportunity for Arnold's former teammates to come back to Iowa City for a weekend would be the February 18, 2017 game against Illinois. There was a lot of work to do to make that a reality.

We needed to continue to sell the TFL shirts, get them licensed with the University of Iowa and make them available at sporting goods stores in Iowa City and Coralville, market the "White Out" idea with press releases and advertising, schedule media interviews, and get everything cleared by the university, among other details.

"From the time Talk To Me Technologies donated the device to Kenny, to Ben putting the shirt together, to the planning to get things together for a 'White Out,' it was a short period of time," said Brookins. "A lot of things needed to get done and yet, it got done. The way I see it is when God is in it, everything falls into place ... and God was in it."

We also needed to get a much larger inventory of shirts available, and a couple of Arnold's "Teammates For Life" quietly stepped in to help provide the funding for that.

Ultimately, there was a tremendous turnout of Arnold's former teammates who arrived in Iowa City that weekend and agreed to sign autographs for Hawk fans at long tables lined up on the concourse of Carver-Hawkeye Arena, starting when the doors opened at 11:30 a.m. prior to the 1 p.m. tipoff.

The University of Iowa provided a replica of a 1980 game program cover for each fan to have autographed as they walked through the line and met their favorite Hawkeye basketball players of that era.

It was a beautiful February day in Eastern Iowa with bright sunshine and temperatures in the 50s. As Emily and I stood outside the arena with four of our children – Carly, Molly, Ben and Sophie – we weren't wearing coats, which highlighted the fact that we were each wearing our TFL shirts. The excitement was building before the doors were unlocked and the lines outside the arena continued to grow. The game was sold out.

When the doors were opened at 11:30 a.m., fans poured into the arena and immediately stood in line to get autographs

118

from the former Hawks who were seated at the tables. Former Iowa players like Gannon, Hansen, Greg Stokes, Jess Settles, King, Craig Anderson, Todd Berkenpas, Lester, Waite, Brookins and Henry visited with each fan as people walked through, smiling ear-to-ear and sharing memories. The line stretched around the concourse as far as you could see.

Almost all of the fans were wearing white shirts … and many of them were wearing the TFL shirts that we had designed to honor Kenny.

"We were not surprised at all about the fan support," said Henry. "Iowa fans never forget the Hawkeyes. We were so happy to be there to sign autographs and share stories. For us, it was a way to give back and say 'thank you' to all the fans. It was a very special day, but that's who Iowa fans are."

As I stood in line with my children that day, I looked at the former Hawks signing autographs and how proud they were. I looked at the seemingly endless line of Iowa fans in line and how excited they were. Then I looked at my kids and I felt so grateful that they were a part of this day … and that they were all old enough to remember it for a long time.

This was something special that, while we had discussed it as a possibility, it was even greater than expected when it became a reality. The pride that I felt in having a hand in this exceptional day was impossible to quantify.

"To have the support of the university and all the guys was awesome," said Brookins. "When I sit back and think about it, all of it took place with only a handful of guys behind the scenes making it happen, it's incredible. Then all the guys came together to be a part of it and to do it for Kenny. It was magic ... God's work."

After signing autographs for an hour, the former Hawks took their seats in the arena ... Emily, our kids and I were lucky to be seated among them. I had a few of my siblings in attendance with their families and I had secured a ticket for my dad to sit with my family close to the court.

We watched the current Hawkeye team warm up before the game. Each of the players was wearing a TFL shirt again, to honor Arnold and his teammates. It was wonderful to observe Ben seeing all of this unfold, knowing that it started out in our kitchen when he initially designed the shirts on our laptop.

"That was incredible walking into the arena, seeing everybody wearing the shirts, sitting down and watching the players warm up in them, and then seeing the sold-out crowd slowly build a sea of white for tipoff," said Ben. "Everyone came together to support Kenny and I think that just shows the type of people Kenny and these guys are."

Prior to the game, I took another minute to soak it all in. I looked around the arena, packed with fans wearing white, including waves of the white TFL shirts, displaying so much love for Kenny Arnold. I looked at Arnold's former team-mates, Streif (former trainer), Sandy Blom (former manager), Jackie Reed (close friend) Johnie Butler (former coach) and they were all so happy, sharing stories, laughs and memories. I looked at Emily and our four oldest kids – our youngest, two-year-old Leo, was with Emily's parents – and I was so thrilled to enjoy this moment with them.

Then I looked at my dad, who was beaming with pride. He was 92 years old, wearing a TFL shirt and as happy as he could be. As he clapped along with the Iowa Fight Song, my mind went back to those days in our living room when I was a young boy, watching the Hawkeye games on the Iowa Television Network ... cheering for Iowa together and sharing the joy and pain of the wins and losses. I thought about my mom, who had passed away eight years earlier after a battle with breast cancer. Mom was a tremendous Hawkeye fan too and I knew that somehow, she was looking down at this scene with a big smile on her face. Because today, we had somehow stumbled into helping create an atmosphere at a game in Carver-Hawkeye Arena that was unique, memorable and meaningful.

It was one moment when everything came together in a way that was well beyond my hopes.

Brookins was right, it *was* magic.

There was a "game watch" party scheduled at Arnold's nursing home that day. The staff and residents – along with friends of Arnold's who were attending – planned to watch the game on TV together.

The large, flat-screen television in the common area where the "watch party" was taking place was donated by another one of Arnold's former teammates, who quietly made the contribution. Another outstanding example of Arnold's "Teammates For Life" stepping in and helping people out.

"It was great having Kenny watching on TV and I knew it meant the world to him to see all the shirts," said Henry. "He was so happy. To see him celebrated on TV, it gave him almost 'celebrity' status at the nursing home."

Several photos were posted on Arnold's Facebook page throughout the day, showing Arnold enjoying a wonderful afternoon of celebrating the former Hawkeye's positive spirit and strength. Arnold had to be overcome with joy seeing so many Hawkeye fans wearing shirts bearing his name and number.

At halftime of the game, the University of Iowa recognized each of the former Hawks who were in attendance and had them walk out to center court. Each one of them received a wonderful ovation from the 15,500 fans in attendance as they were introduced by the PA announcer.

"Assistant Coach from 1978 to 1980, a native of Vicksburg, Mississippi, please welcome back Johnie Butler!

"He was a forward from 1978 to 1981, hailing from Elgin, Illinois, please welcome home Mike 'Tree' Henry!" The crowd began chanting "TREEEEE!"

"A guard who played from 1981 to 1984, from Independence, Missouri, welcome home Waymond King!

"A forward who played from 1981 to 1984, from Madison, Wisconsin, please welcome home Craig Anderson!

"From Hamilton, Ohio, a center who played from 1982 through 1985, welcome home one-half of the 'Twin Towers,' Greg Stokes!

"A guard from 1982 to 1985, originally from Mapleton, Iowa, welcome home Todd Berkenpas!

"A homegrown center who played from 1978 to 1981, an Iowa City native, welcome home Steve Waite!

"A forward who played from 1978 to 1981, from Cleveland, Ohio, welcome home Vince Brookins!

"A guard who played from 1980 to 1983, from Des Moines, Iowa, welcome home Bobby Hansen!

"A guard who played from 1977 to 1980, from Chicago, Illinois, welcome home Ronnie Lester!" At this point, the entire crowd was standing and roaring.

"A forward who played from 1994 to 1999, from Winfield, Iowa, welcome home Jess Settles!"

At that time, on the big screen above center court, there was a photo of Arnold, Henry and Lester, holding the TFL shirts. And the PA announcer had one more former player to honor.

"Finally, not in attendance this afternoon, a guard for the Hawkeyes from 1979 to 1982, from Chicago, Illinois, a Hawkeye for life ... number 30 ... Kenny Arnold!"

The crowd went crazy. Everyone was standing, cheering and many were caught up in the emotion of it all. This wasn't just a time to honor these former Hawkeye greats for their countless successes on the court, but rather, a time to recognize their winning spirit and support that has continued for more than 30 years for their teammate.

As the former Hawks in attendance walked off the floor, the pep band played The Iowa Fight Song and the ovation continued.

I had attended many games at Carver-Hawkeye Arena through the years, but I had never heard the crowd make so much noise for an extended period for something that was unrelated to the actual game being played.

"We all have egos, so it's nice to be remembered," said Henry. "But it was really a way for us to say 'thank you' to the fans, as well. It's a mutual love affair. It's always great to come back and see everyone, but also to say 'thank you' for the support."

"I know Kenny totally appreciated it," said Hansen. "His situation has been one thing that's kept our team together. We all want him to live a good life and without pain."

Iowa lost the game that day to Illinois, 70-66. But the defeat could not touch the positive feelings that were generated.

"It was special to have the guys come back because we were all super close," said Henry. "It's comforting to know that you can pick up the phone and the guys are there ... and they care about Kenny. The love we share together is tremendous and really helps keep Kenny going. He's so happy to be remembered and cared about. All in all, it was a tremendous day and event."

––––––––––––––––

Almost six weeks later, on March 30, 2017, Hawkeye senior Peter Jok competed in the College Basketball 3-Point Championship held at Grand Canyon University in Phoenix, Arizona. This contest was part of the festivities of the Final Four. Between rounds and after the competition, Jok wore his long-sleeve TFL shirt, honoring Kenny Arnold on national TV.

Jok won the men's competition. A fitting tribute at a Final Four event, 37 years after Arnold had helped lead the Hawkeyes to that pinnacle of college basketball.

CHAPTER 9

Kenny Returns to Iowa City

Fry Fest is billed as "The World's Largest Hawkeye Tradeshow" and takes place inside the Exhibition Hall of the Coralville Marriott every year during the first home football weekend of the season. The event was named after legendary Iowa football coach Hayden Fry, who was busy turning the Hawkeye football program into a Big Ten power in the early 1980s while Coach Olson was doing the same with the basketball program.

In 2017, the tradeshow took place on Friday, September 1. Approximately 20,000 Iowa fans would come through the aisles of this event, viewing items at more than 60 booths. Everything black-and-gold would be displayed, from Hawkeye clothing and artwork to games and collectibles.

The Kenny Arnold Foundation had just been created, so Henry reserved a booth at Fry Fest in an effort to generate donations for the foundation, which would then donate funds to various cancer charities, and donations for Arnold's care, as well. At the booth, there would be TFL shirts for sale, along with TFL bracelets and posters. And there were donation boxes front and center for anyone who was willing to help Arnold specifically.

But the biggest news was that Henry was able to bring Arnold along for this trip, the first time that Kenny had been out of Chicago in more than a year.

––––––––––––––––

The Thursday evening before Fry Fest at about 5:30 p.m., Henry, Brookins and Arnold arrive at their room at The Marriott.

"Let's give him a bath," Henry says to Brookins, a few minutes after getting settled into the room. "We've got to get him cleaned up." Brookins agrees.

"Sound good to you?" Henry asks Arnold, who nods.

Henry lifts Arnold from behind his shoulders, while Brookins takes him by the legs. They carry Arnold to the bathroom and get him undressed. As Henry sits at the edge of the tub, holding Arnold upright as he is seated in the tub, Brookins starts the water and gets it to the right temperature. Brookins also dumps the liquid soap into the tub while the water is running … and they all soon discover that he may have overdone that task.

There are a lot of bubbles and Arnold is getting too slippery for Henry to both hold and wash up with a washcloth.

"Hold him for a second," says Henry. Brookins takes Henry's place at the side of the tub, holding Arnold upright. Henry takes off his own pants and socks, steps into the tub behind Arnold to hold him up, while both Henry and Brookins do their best to get their friend cleaned up.

As the six-foot-nine Henry and six-foot-five Brookins are working feverishly to get the six-foot-two Arnold clean and not physically hurt him, the bubbles and water are flying around the hotel bathtub. Sweat is just *pouring* off the foreheads of Henry and Brookins in what Henry later described as "just another adventure you couldn't plan."

At the height of the chaos, the three men just start laughing. "It was our way to get through it," said Henry.

After the bath, they get Arnold dressed and back into bed.

"We'll go down the hall, grab something to eat quick and get something for you," Henry says to Arnold, who nods. The caregiver they hired for the weekend is expected to arrive in a couple of hours.

Henry and Brookins leave the room and begin walking down the hallway.

"You do this kind of thing all the time?" Brookins asks Henry.

"Yes," Henry says. "This is what it takes to help take care of him. It's physical work and while you're doing it, you're trying not to hurt him. And it's also emotional because you realize how much he's changed and what his limits are."

Ben and I went to Iowa City for the weekend, and we worked at the booth all day on that Friday. Fans of all ages swarmed our corner of the hall. Of course, it didn't hurt that former Hawks like Lester, Brookins, Henry and Waite were also working at the booth.

All morning, fans were asking, "Is Kenny here?" We let them know he would be making an appearance soon.

Sometime around 11 a.m., Brookins and Henry walked upstairs to the room where Arnold was staying. A caregiver was present to help him throughout the weekend. They lifted Arnold up into his wheelchair and brought him down to the exhibit hall.

Arnold was wearing a black-and-gold Iowa baseball cap with a few gray hairs poking out above his ears and he was covered up in a black-and-gold Hawkeye blanket. His left arm was uncovered, though, allowing him to wave and shake hands with people as Brookins pushed him along in his chair.

As Arnold was wheeled into the hall, you could hear a murmur among the fans. People formed a new line almost immediately to gather around Arnold and share their greetings with him. One by one, people reached out their hand to his and made comments, shared memories, took photos and shook his left hand. "Thanks for coming to Iowa," said one man. "Hey Kenny … we're thinking of you!" said another.

The pain in Arnold's hip was too great for him to sit up in his chair for much more than 30 minutes, but he had a big smile for every single person who shared a kind word or even a nod in his direction.

This was the first time that Ben had a chance to meet Arnold in person. I introduced my son to Arnold and the two shared a couple of big smiles. Watching these two interact was such a proud moment for me ... and it was even more special because Ben was about the same age as I was back when I pretended to be Arnold on my driveway as a boy. I had a photo taken that day of the three of us – Ben, Kenny and me – and it remains one of my favorites. Eventually, I had this photo framed professionally with a little plaque on it that reads, "Teammates For Life."

I knew that Arnold grew up as a White Sox fan, so I teased him about how good the Cubs had become, as the defending World Series champions ... and Arnold shook his head and smiled about that, too.

As the crowd began to dissipate a little bit, I showed Arnold a few highlights on my phone from a game that he played in for the Hawks in the early 1980s. He was focused on the video. When the young Kenny Arnold made a perimeter jump shot, I asked him, "What could you have done with a three-point line (which didn't come into college basketball until after Arnold's career was over)?" Arnold's smile grew as large as it had been all morning, his eyebrows were raised and he nodded repeatedly. He KNEW that the three-pointer would've been just one more weapon in his arsenal back then. And we both laughed.

At that moment, a local television station came over to do a segment on the "Teammates For Life" concept and the return to Iowa City for Arnold. Brookins, Henry and Waite were situated for the reporter. Then Brookins grabbed Ben and had him stand next to him for the entire story. It was fun to watch ... and Kenny's smile never left his face.

At around 11:30 a.m., Henry and Brookins wheeled Arnold out of the hall and back up to his room, so he could lay back down on his bed and get comfortable again. The pain in his hip was relentless.

Fans waved to him on his way out ... and Arnold grinned and waved right back.

"Iowa fans are great fans," said Coach Butler, who made the trip from Chicago to be there for the weekend. "They've been extremely generous and supportive of Kenny. And they have a long history of being supportive of African-Americans, all the way back to Duke Slater (who was an All-American football player for the Hawks in 1921)."

Two hours later, there was a panel discussion scheduled in the hall that was to feature the 1980 Hawkeyes who had made it to the Final Four. Brookins had gone back to Arnold's room and wheeled him back down for this event.

"Kenny is able to still feel the support and well-wishes," said Brookins. "We used to say the Iowa fans would always recognize and support you. But now when you're 60 years old and they still recognize and support you, like they did then, it's amazing."

There was an extremely large crowd forming for this panel discussion, which was the featured event on the day's schedule. Arnold sat in the front row, with Jackie Reed, Ben and I next to him. In the seats directly behind Arnold were Kirk Speraw, a current Iowa basketball assistant coach who played and coached at Iowa during Arnold's career, Coach Butler, Berkenpas and Brookins. There were hundreds of Iowa fans, both seated and standing, as the discussion began.

Up on the stage, former Iowa Sports Information Director Phil Haddy was the emcee, while former Hawks Lester, Waite, Henry, Boyle and Hansen sat at a long table, each with a microphone to answer questions and share stories.

After Haddy introduced all the other Hawkeyes in attendance, he introduced Arnold. "It is wonderful to have Kenny here and he's an inspiration to all of us," said Haddy. The entire crowd stood up and applauded with enthusiasm for an extended period. I looked at Arnold and he was clearly touched and very happy.

"I think one of the coolest moments of my life was when they introduced Kenny and everybody rose to their feet and cheered for him," said my son Ben. "That gave me goosebumps."

Henry said that for Arnold to see so many of his former teammates and all the fans that day, it was very uplifting. "He really enjoyed seeing the fans," said Henry. "That was such a very special day. For him to actually get back to Iowa City really meant a lot to him."

As his teammates told stories to the crowd, Arnold was listening intently to every word. He smiled with pride as Boyle said, "Kenny Arnold took over at the point guard and did a wonderful job running the team." And he nodded as Henry thanked the fans for all the notes they had written to Arnold on his Facebook page and said that it means the world to Arnold when he sees those comments.

Toward the end of the discussion, Henry explained what he thinks makes this group of former teammates so special. "One of the great things when we all talk to each other – to every one of these guys – every conversation ends with an 'I love you,'" he said. "We truly care about each other and I think that's the thing that's so special about our group. And we feel the same way about you fans. I can't say how many people today have done that for Kenny and that will carry him for a long time. So, just a big thank you to everybody."

The next day, on Saturday, September 2, the Hawkeye football team had its season opener at 11 a.m. The opponent was Wyoming, which featured one of the nation's top quarterbacks in Josh Allen. It was a beautiful autumn day with a bright blue sky and temperatures in the 70s.

Ben and I received our tickets the night before from Brookins. I believe that these seats belonged to Iowa basketball coach Fran McCaffery, or at least that's what we were told. Given that we were sitting around the 50-yard-line, about halfway up the stands on the pressbox side of the field, it wasn't hard to believe. There may not be better seats in Kinnick Stadium than where we were sitting that afternoon. Sitting next to us were Lester and Reed. We had a blast watching the game together.

At different times in the first quarter, fans would reach out to Lester to take a photo or just wish him the best. As always, he was gracious and genuine in his communication with the Iowa fans.

We had been instructed to head down to the field level at the end of the first quarter, as the 1980 team would be recognized on the field at halftime. The team had invited Ben and me to join them and we couldn't pass up this once-in-a-lifetime opportunity.

As the first quarter came to a close, Reed, Lester, Ben and I stood to leave our seats. As we were walking up the steps to the exit, the PA announcer mentioned the first-ever "Wave" by the Kinnick Stadium fans to the children and families in the top floor of the University of Iowa Stead Family Children's Hospital. So, we waved to the hospital with the rest of the 68,075 fans in attendance as the Hawkeye fans started the greatest new tradition in college sports.

When we arrived down on the field level, we found Henry, Brookins and Arnold. Arnold was in the back of a golf cart, facing out. Again, he was wearing his black-and-gold Iowa baseball cap and covered up in his Hawkeye blanket. He had his left arm exposed so he could shake our hands.

Brookins told us that it was a little rough for Arnold to get to Kinnick and that they would take him right back to his room at the Marriott when the halftime event was completed. The pain in Arnold's hip made these kinds of extended periods of sitting up in his wheelchair almost too much to bear.

"It's tough to see Kenny in the shape he's in now when you think about where he was as an athlete," said Brookins. "But it's a blessing to have him with us. To see him at Fry Fest and all the fans recognizing him and for the team to be there surrounding him, it was emotional.

"It was emotional at the hotel, getting him ready to get to Kinnick. All those things made it almost spiritual because of the things that lined up for him to be able to go through it. I look at all of it and say, 'This is God at work.'"

Streif, the legendary former trainer at Iowa, was also down on the field level. He offered support and words of encouragement to Arnold, and Arnold was definitely very happy to see him.

Other former Hawkeyes began to emerge down on the field level, including Hansen, Darsee, Mike Arens, Greg Boyle, Waite and Kevin Boyle.

Ben and I stood there, right behind the black painted grass of the north end zone, as the Iowa football team drove directly toward us right before halftime. Nate Stanley threw a perfect 27-yard strike to tight end Noah Fant with 22 seconds remaining in the second quarter to give Iowa a 14-3 halftime lead. Ben was filled with adrenaline as he ran back and forth, cheering and pumping his fists for the Hawks. This ground-level, end zone view of a score at Kinnick Stadium was something new for both of us.

Immediately after the two teams exited the field at half-time, we were led out to the end zone with the members of the 1980 Final Four team.

Twelve-and-a-half years earlier, Henry was carrying Arnold over his shoulder into the McKale Center in Tucson, Arizona, searching for their former coach, Lute Olson, and hoping for some answers about Arnold's deteriorating health. On *this* sunny day, however, Henry and Arnold rode out onto the Kinnick Stadium grass, sitting side-by-side on the back of a golf cart, waiting to hear the cheers from 68,000 of their most loyal fans. Indeed, the journey to get to this point had been quite a ride.

The golf cart carrying Arnold and Henry was driven to its place with the rest of their former teammates ... and Ben and me. This situation would've been difficult for even my 10-year-old self to dream up. My son and I were standing in the end zone of Kinnick Stadium, being recognized along with the 1980 Final Four team. Surreal.

There we were, all lined up, as the Kinnick Stadium crowd gave a rousing ovation: Brookins, Henry, Arnold, Speraw, me, Ben, Reed, Hansen, Darsee, Arens, Greg Boyle, Coach Butler, Lester, Kevin Boyle and Waite.

The PA announcer welcomed back the members of the most successful Hawkeye basketball team of the past four decades and concluded with, "From the 1980 men's basketball team, a true Hawkeye, Kenny Arnold!" The noise that 68,000 people can make when they are cheering together is something to behold … it was like the front row at a rock concert. But as they cheered, Arnold raised his left arm from under his blanket and waved. The big screen showed him waving and the crowd took their noise up a notch.

Immediate goosebumps for me. And I think anyone else who was close enough to see the expression on Arnold's face. Absolute joy.

"At halftime, just to be able to wave to the crowd and hear the roar of the crowd," said Henry. "In talking to Kenny, the overriding feeling was that it was a great way to see all the teammates and fans, and say 'thank you' to everybody. It was a really special time."

As the golf cart wheeled out of the end zone and back into the exit area, the crowd continued to roar. While the celebration was meant for the entire 1980 team, there was little doubt who the fans were targeting with their cheers. The man of the hour was Kenny Arnold … and tens of thousands of Hawkeye fans were letting him hear it.

Prior to the Fry Fest weekend, Henry programmed a button on Arnold's speech device with a very personal message from Arnold. When Arnold pressed the button, it said, "My name is Kenny Arnold. I played basketball for the Iowa Hawkeyes. We won the Big Ten Conference in 1979 and made it to the Final Four in 1980. I've had several health problems in the last 30 years, including a brain tumor and multiple strokes.

I'm a fighter so I'm still here but I couldn't do it by myself. I needed a very special group of people helping me, supporting me and caring for me … my Teammates For Life. I want to thank you all for everything you've done for me. You haven't forgotten me and I won't forget you. To the best fans in the world, Go Hawks! To all my Teammates For Life, I love you."

CHAPTER 10

The Hawkeye Basketball Family

Adversity is fascinating. It can rip things apart. Or it can bring people together and make their bonds stronger.

"When you look back, we had so much adversity on that 1980 team," said Streif. "Things went wrong that made it very tough, but we grew stronger and more positive. Kenny was a leader to keep everyone together and keep moving things forward in a positive way. He's been such a uniter ... even with his health issues, he's still bringing these guys together."

Streif is absolutely correct. As I've gotten to know this group the last few years, the former Hawks have held several different reunions and the common theme each time has been Arnold. Conversations focus on Arnold's health, happiness and reasons to remain hopeful. And now, nearly 40 years since many of these men played basketball in Iowa City, the Hawkeye fans continue to show up to offer their appreciation and support for a group of guys they cheered for every Thursday and Saturday way back when.

"Our opponents from other schools, they all thought Iowa was something special," said Henry. "They could see the support we had from the fan base. They see the help we've had with Kenny and it's something that is really rare. The people of Iowa don't forget us. Anybody who's worn the black-and-gold is always remembered in the state of Iowa and it's something special. We don't take that for granted at all."

Streif agreed. "I don't think this story could happen at any other school in the nation," he said. "The fans have always stepped up to help Kenny, long after his playing days were over. His teammates all got involved. It says an awful lot about Kenny's teammates and the fans of this state ... and how Lute brought in guys of high character. That's what makes this so special."

Coach Olson's policy of only recruiting student-athletes who would fit in as people with his current roster ended up creating a family atmosphere that has stood the test of time. Forty years later and this group – this Hawkeye basketball *family* – is still close.

"Through the whole recruiting process, Coach Olson would always ask us about a recruit after a visit, 'Will he fit in with our group? Will he be a good citizen? Is he a person of character?'" said Hansen. "All of this created a family environment that was positive and encouraging."

"It was not a mistake that we had good people," said Kevin Boyle. "There were better players out there – some great athletes – but Lute wouldn't jeopardize his program for that to get a prima donna. It was important to get along on the court and off the court.

"Lute would tell us 'You're going to spend four years with your teammates but you're going to be friends for 40 years.' And that's really been true."

One future All-American and first-round NBA draft pick was on a recruiting visit to Iowa City as a high school senior and tested Coach Olson's policy.

"This guy was really arrogant," said Henry. "He was complaining at dinner about the food and the service ... and being a jerk about it. It was supposed to be a visit for the entire weekend, but Lute sent him home early on Saturday. Lute only wanted people who would fit in and get along. It didn't matter how good a *player* was, Lute would quit recruiting them if they didn't fit in as *people*."

Waite reiterated the importance of Coach Olson's practice of recruiting people with strong character and similar values. "That's why we played well together and had such good chemistry," he said. "We may come from different parts of the country ... some from rural areas and others from big cities, but we all showed the same values. And that all came from Lute."

Lester added that the team's chemistry played a large role. "You've got to be in tune with your teammates and be unselfish," he said. "It helps if you like the guys you play with. Thank God we had a guy like Coach Olson who wouldn't recruit bad apples. Being on the same page, wanting the same things and being unselfish helped lead to our success."

Gannon recalled how well the team handled adversity, in part because they truly cared for each other. "We were a group of close-knit guys who never gave up on each other," he said. "No one panicked (when Lester was injured). We all asked, 'What can we do?' It was a tribute to Coach Olson, Coach Rosborough, Coach McAndrews and the way they built the team."

As time passed for these men during the next four decades, they continued to face difficult circumstances head on, without feeling hopeless. And they continued to ask, "What can we do?" A tribute to the lessons learned as basketball players at Iowa, the leadership of Coach Olson and his staff, and the character of the young men who were recruited to be part of a team all those years ago.

"We honestly are a band of brothers who care for each other way beyond basketball," said Henry. "And because of what Kenny's been through, we came together even closer. As the years have passed, we talk less about basketball with each other. Kenny's situation has taught us how fragile life can be.

"You can play basketball anywhere. It's the other stuff that makes the difference."

142

When Krafcisin thinks about the "other stuff," he knows that he made the right move, transferring to Iowa for his final three seasons. "I think about the impact all the guys have had on me and how life is better for all of us being a part of each other's lives," he said. "It's like the brothers you never had. Luckily, the Lord was looking after me and I transferred from North Carolina to Iowa. There was nothing better than those years at Iowa.

"We had an incredibly special group where we all liked each other, which helped spearhead us to play well and succeed. Whenever we get together now, it's a magical thing."

Gannon added how much he appreciates what that Hawkeye team enjoyed together. "It was a family environment that made you really feel comfortable," he said. "I wish every kid who goes to Iowa could have the same experience that we had. When you feel that the guy next to you is more important than you are ... then, he'll treat you the same way. Pretty soon, you've built something that's monumental."

Gannon is exactly right. Coach Olson and his staff built something monumental, all right. The philosophy of bringing together young men of high character helped lead the basketball team to greater heights than most observers would've guessed was possible, even in the face of some extreme adversity on the court. As a result, the Hawkeye squad was consistently greater than the sum of its parts, which is the aspiration of every successful team.

The enduring, and most significant, outcome of the coaching staff's resolve is that this collection of people would continue to face tough circumstances with courage and grace, *off the court* – supporting each other like a family – for the next several decades.

Through the years, I have played – and coached – hundreds of basketball games and participated in thousands of practices. While I didn't play at a Division 1 university, I did play a little bit at a small college (Buena Vista University in Storm Lake, Iowa) at the Division III level. Then, in my 20s, I was the varsity boys high school coach at Storm Lake High School for six seasons. Since then, I have coached several youth basketball teams as my children have participated.

All that experience has taught me many lessons, but one thing is true of most every basketball team: If the best players on the team are its hardest workers and most selfless players, those characteristics will naturally flow down through the rest of the unit, which helps build a chemistry that is team-oriented and strong. Players will make sacrifices – big and small – for the good of the team because that becomes the expectation. Nobody is bigger than the team.

The opposite is also true: If the best players on the team are ego driven, selfish and willing to take short cuts – and the coaching staff accepts this – then *this attitude* will permeate throughout the rest of the team, as well. Once that snowball starts rolling down the hill, it's awfully difficult to stop. There will almost certainly be in-fighting, finger-pointing and a litany of excuses for why things don't work out, but it all starts at the top. What will the coaching staff prioritize and demand from the team, including its top players? And what will the leaders of the team be willing to sacrifice for the entire group to succeed?

I've discussed many times with basketball coaches how there are two common types of basketball players: those who would rather score 20 points in a game but lose ... and those who would rather score two points in a game but *win*. Obviously, if you have a roster full of the former, your team will never come close to its potential.

However, when you have a team full of players who don't care about individual accolades and awards, but are instead focused on the *team's* success, those are the squads that reach their potential – whether that means 25 wins or five wins – and they are the most enjoyable teams to play for, to coach and to watch.

As an Iowan, I know that this is the type of team that Hawkeye fans love to support and will show up at a pep rally at midnight – with 15,000 others – to express our full appreciation.

The Hawkeye teams of the late 1970s and early 1980s were full of these types of basketball players. Guys who would dive for loose balls, make the extra pass, hustle defensively and protect the basketball. It is clear, looking back, that Coach Olson and his staff prioritized this type of play ... and recruited this kind of person.

Lester was an All-American basketball player. He was so talented that, despite a pair of injuries to his right knee during his senior season, he was drafted into the NBA with the 10th overall pick in the spring of 1980. When Lester was injured in December of his final season at Iowa, he dedicated his efforts and rehabilitation to return to the court to help his teammates at the end of the season.

When Iowa earned an invitation to the NCAA Tournament that season, did the Hawkeyes' all-time leading scorer feel that it was time for him to step forward and take control of the team's offense? Actually, no, he didn't. "I had missed so much time and didn't want to get in the way of the team," said Lester. "I wanted to blend in. I didn't want to come back and mess up what the team had going. I just wanted to fit in and help as much as I could."

It wasn't just a good line, either. During the five games that Lester played in the NCAA Tourney in 1980, Iowa's All-American was FOURTH on the team in shot attempts. But he continued to distribute the ball extremely well, with 29 assists and only seven turnovers. Lester played 39 minutes of the pressure-packed victory over Georgetown and finished with nine assists and zero turnovers.

Now, *that* is leadership. It's exactly the type of selflessness from a highly-decorated athlete that sets the tone for the entire team. This was the type of culture that had been established at Iowa, from Coach Olson to Lester all the way down the entire roster.

There were many successes that came out of that culture of making individual sacrifices for the good of the team. Certainly, the trip to the Final Four was one. I would contend that this group's selfless response – time after time – to assisting Kenny Arnold in his times of need the last 30-plus years has been another.

———————————

One more significant characteristic that has been obvious as I've gotten the chance to know many of these former Hawks is the lack of ego they exhibit. Considering their high levels of success, it is a truly noticeable trait. For example, both Lester and Hansen have won NBA championships as players – and Lester has won several more as an executive – but you could have hours of conversations with either of them and never know it.

I've seen a room full of people watch the end of the Georgetown game together and I watched Waite turn his head, almost embarrassed, as his younger self made the game-winning shot. Gannon and Brookins often turn to a self-deprecating sense of humor ... and so does everyone else, really. After having dozens of conversations with almost every former Hawk from that era, I have found them all to be very humble and unassuming.

It's unusual, I think, given all the adoration these guys received as teenagers and young adults. But Waymond King said that it all goes back to their common character traits.

"We were a team of guys who had to work hard and not take anything for granted," he said. "We would dig in, work hard and scrap. The fellowship and brotherhood came not just from the off-season and preseason work, but all the sacrifices you have to make in order to be competitive in this sport.

"I love these guys. When we get together now, there is a mutual love, admiration and respect there that won't ever change. It's a bond based on a shared experience. It was a magical time that was beyond a typical college experience. We were young, but we had the proper amount of respect for the adulation. We stayed grounded and kept each other close."

———————

Today, the Hawkeye basketball program sees Arnold as an inspiration for its current student-athletes to emulate.

In the spring of 2017, the Iowa men's basketball program added a special award to be given annually to a player at the end-of-the-season banquet. The "Kenny Arnold Hawkeye Spirit Award" is presented to the Hawkeye who exemplifies Kenny's spirit of leadership, character, courage, determination and poise. This player inspires his teammates to be their very best in spite of the odds.

"When I see this award that is named in Kenny's honor, it makes my heart warm, it really does," said Streif.

———————

Almost 40 years later, Coach McAndrews still holds these Hawkeyes in extremely high regard. "I've been around basketball a lot and I hear the terms 'team' and 'family' thrown around a lot," he said. "But this bunch has stayed together throughout the years and has taken care of Kenny, and really looked out for him. Everybody has bent over backwards for

Kenny because they really love him. They are 'Teammates For Life.'

"I get teary-eyed and emotional talking about that team because I have such fond memories. I feel so fortunate to have coached those guys."

Coach McAndrews added that the relationship with Hawkeye fans has added a special element to the family atmosphere of the program. "It's amazing what the people of Iowa have done for Kenny," he said. "They are the best fans anywhere. The joy in life is in giving, whether it's time, love or money. This story has all of that."

While he lives in Florida now and enjoys the time he spends on the golf course, Coach McAndrews' affinity for the Hawkeye basketball program remains strong. "If I had a young son right now looking for a place to play basketball, I would send him to Iowa," he said. "The snow is seasonal ... but the fan support and how the people stick together is phenomenal, and that's *not* seasonal."

At noon, Henry arrives at Arnold's room at Symphony of Morgan Park nursing home. Arnold is in bed, covered in his black-and-gold Hawkeye blanket. Henry takes a seat in the wheelchair next to Arnold's bed.

A nurse arrives within a couple of minutes with the day's lunch and puts it on the tray table next to Arnold's bed, to his left. The day's lunch is pepper steak, rice, a cup of fruit punch, a carton of milk and a small piece of chocolate cake.

While Arnold uses a remote to adjust the head of his bed up to a 45-degree angle, Henry cuts up the pepper steak into manageable bites for his friend.

Henry sits next to Arnold, who struggles to keep the steak on the fork and move it to his mouth. Arnold's pride doesn't allow him to ask for help, but he's not having much success with his lunch. Henry always lets Arnold try before offering, but after a few failed attempts, he takes over.

"I got it," said Henry. And Arnold nods.

Nothing else needed to be said. Henry scoops food up onto the fork and lifts it to Arnold's mouth.

After a few bites, Arnold reaches for his cup of fruit punch and sips it through a straw.

Then, Henry begins to feed his friend again.

This Hawkeye basketball family is proud of what it's achieving as the "Teammates For Life" concept continues to grow.

"There's nothing like 'Teammates For Life,'" said Coach Butler, who visits Arnold frequently enough at the nursing home that several staff members there thought for a while that he was Arnold's brother. "When you're down and out, just need a handshake, hug or comforting word, that's what life's all about.

"It means everything to Kenny. He's got all kinds of Hawkeye memorabilia on his walls in his room. Every time he goes out to therapy, he wears his Iowa sweats and Iowa cap."

Brookins reflected on the battle that his good friend has been fighting for more than 30 years. "I feel bad that Kenny's life has been challenged with having to experience cancer and it changed the course of his life," he said. "But I feel blessed to be a part of a group that tries to help build the quality of his life."

Michael Payne was a freshman at Iowa when Arnold was a senior, and he played basketball overseas until the mid-1990s, but they have remained connected. "I always looked up to Kenny as a leader, but since becoming involved in the 'Teammates For Life,' he's kind of grounded me," said Payne. "There are things you don't take for granted, like your health and your mobility. Don't sweat the little things. Be grateful for your health and the things you do have. To worry about some of the things we worry about, it isn't worth it. Be grateful for the friends and people in your life who will stand by you, come hell or high water."

Waite said that the effect on Arnold is obvious. "I know Kenny feels great about the support he's had from his team-mates," he said. "When you're with him, you see his eyes light up and his smile breaks out. With what he's been through and what he's going through now, friendships and teammates are critical."

"'Teammates For Life' is a way for all of us to band together and do something good and very special," said Henry. "It sets an example as we try to do different things for Kenny. It can be overwhelming for an individual to do these things, but if we work together, we can make a difference.

"It doesn't always take a lot of money, either. Taking the time to stop and visit someone can make a tremendous difference. When everybody does a little bit, it can have a big impact."

The "Teammates For Life" story has been followed by friends and fans of the Hawkeyes all over the world. Their former play-by-play announcer, Bob Hogue, has followed the details via Facebook. "It's a story of extraordinary love among teammates, the courage of Kenny, and the loyalty and follow-through by Tree," he said.

"The love between them and how their teammates have stayed together, reached out and shown their love and support in every way they can is amazing."

———————

"Because of the quality of people we played with at Iowa, they still want to do whatever they can to help Kenny," said Lester. "Basketball brought us all together at that time, but as you get older, you remember your teammates and the camaraderie … and you always have those memories.

"I don't know why Kenny decided to go to Iowa, but when he made that decision, it was probably the best decision he could've ever made."

CHAPTER 11

Progress, Inspiration and Peace

The chronic pain Arnold suffers was evident for all of us who spent time with him at Fry Fest in early September of 2017. But there was good news just around the corner for Arnold, thanks to all the efforts of his "Teammates For Life," including former Hawks, coaches, fans and friends who banded together to try to help the former Iowa basketball player.

Enough money had been raised through shirt sales, donations and the Go Fund Me account to finally get Arnold started on physical therapy treatments each week at an Athletico facility in Chicago. Athletico, one of the largest employers of physical therapists and athletic trainers in the United States, was founded by Mark Kaufman, who grew up as a Hawkeye fan in the small Southeastern Iowa town of Olds. Kaufman worked with John Streif and the staff at Iowa as a student athletic trainer.

Arnold attended physical therapy sessions once per week for the month of September, but then started going twice per week after that. The goals were to increase his strength, which would also, hopefully, help reduce his pain.

"At his first appointment, Kenny couldn't sit up for more than about 10 seconds on his own," said Henry. "He had no core strength at all. They gave him some core exercises to work on. He worked his way up to sitting for 30 seconds ... then a minute ... and eventually, Kenny could sit up for *five minutes*."

Henry and Arnold meet with the physical therapist, Deb Mahalski, and her assistant, Ed Redmond, at Athletico. Redmond lifts Arnold out of his wheelchair and places Arnold up on the edge of a table. Mahalski wraps a gait belt around Arnold's waist for support as she sits on her knees on the table right behind Arnold. Mahalski supports Arnold, making sure he doesn't fall backwards. Redmond stands in front of Arnold on the side of his right leg, while Henry stands in front on the side of Arnold's left leg. They form a triangle of support for Arnold.

Mahalski coaches Arnold on what to do to sit up. On this day, Henry is perhaps the largest cheerleader in the world, telling his buddy, "You can do this! ... Keep going ... Keep fighting!"

Just like an athlete pushing his teammate to excel and reach his limits, Henry motivates Arnold to find just a little more strength.

As Henry looks at the stopwatch on his phone, he says, "Give me 10 more seconds! ... You can do this!"

When the grimace on Arnold's face grows larger, as his muscles fatigue, he finally loses his balance. As his body slowly falls back toward Mahalski, she supports his weight with her knees as they all help him lean back on the table and relax. Redmond lifts Arnold's legs up and pulls out the table extension to let him rest for a bit.

"Good job!" Henry says, as he and Arnold exchange a fist bump. Both of them smile.

"The expression on his face in those moments is the same as when he would make a big shot in a basketball game," said Henry later. "Kenny takes a lot of pride in reaching those goals and improving his personal bests in those physical therapy sessions."

———————————

Arnold worked on arm curls with his left arm, starting with a one-half pound weight and working his way up to 10 pounds.

He also worked on an exercise bike, using his legs and his left arm. "When Kenny started on the bike, he could go for about a minute," said Henry. "But he kept working and got all the way up to *15 minutes* on the bike. I never dreamed of anything like that for him.

"The numbers don't sound huge, but when you start from scratch, it's so impressive. Kenny is just so competitive and this gave him such a sense of pride."

The improvements were dramatic for Arnold and not just from a physical standpoint. "Just to get out of bed, get dressed and go somewhere to do something, meant so much to Kenny's emotional well-being," said Henry. "Then gaining the physical strength, it has been such an improvement to his quality of life."

Henry described how Arnold couldn't sit at the edge of a table or bed when his physical therapy started, but he improved his core strength to the point that he could *stand* with some assistance for up to two minutes.

"It is a testament to the strength of Kenny's will and the skill of his physical therapist, Deb Mahalski," said Henry. "Deb was extremely knowledgeable and encouraging. She could find a way to keep him pushing to be the best he could be and also cared about him as a person. She's just a tremendous therapist.

"Everybody at Athletico helped Kenny out a lot to be the best he could be and cared about him as a person."

"Kenny does a great job with therapy," said Mahalski. "Mike Henry was able to give Kenny a lot of attention and support, and Kenny really thrived. If he has good, constant stimulation, Kenny does very well."

The improvements that Arnold was able to make in his physical strength also lessened his pain, according to

Henry. "The physical therapy made a big difference with the pain almost immediately," he said. "Kenny's core strength improved and he gained strength in his legs too. All that gave him the ability to reposition himself and roll over on his own, which greatly improved his comfort level.

"It had been almost two years since Kenny had been able to roll himself over, which can be excruciating. Two months into his physical therapy, he was able to roll over on his own."

———————————

Given everything that's taken place in the last 40 years, does Henry stop and think about what his impact has been on Arnold's life?

"It's a mutual thing," said Henry. "Kenny is my brother. I don't give a lot of thought to it. I know that he'd do the same for me. It's what you do for someone you care about. My teammates would all do the same for me. I'm so happy that Kenny is still with us after all these years. It's hard to talk about … I just care about my brother."

Payne shared his feelings about Henry's impact. "Tree has always been a loyal friend," he said. "He and Kenny have always been close. I don't think one could survive without the other. Tree is like Kenny's guardian angel … he's just a saint. Kenny wouldn't still be with us without Tree."

"It's unbelievable," said Waite. "Kenny is like Tree's little brother … or even stronger than that. How Tree feels for Kenny and how Kenny feels for Tree, there's a bond there that's hard to describe. With his time, his commitment and efforts to make Kenny more comfortable, Tree is a role model."

"Tree is an angel," said Carfino. "I think of what Tree has done for Kenny and I cry *every time*."

A brother, a loyal friend, a guardian angel, a role model and a saint. I cannot imagine more powerful words for people to use to describe a teammate. Knowing Mike "Tree" Henry as well as I do now – and seeing first-hand how he walks the walk – I cannot think of any more accurate ways to express who he is and what he represents.

How about Arnold's impact on Henry's life?

"He's the brother I never had," said Henry. "Kenny's an amazing friend. Since he's been sick, he's given me an improved outlook on life. Whatever issue comes up, I try to keep a positive outlook and figure out a solution. I hope we've been able to inspire some other people. He's a tremendous person, friend and teammate. I'm proud to know him and love him."

"Tree has been so good to Kenny, but I think that Tree has gained even more from this than Kenny has," said Streif. "It's been really good for Mike in a lot of ways. He's such a caring person and Kenny keeps him going. It's a two-way street. Kenny helps Mike dearly."

Their former teammates have been impacted in a powerful way, as well.

"I'm not often short for words, but when it comes to Kenny, I have no words for his human spirit," said Carfino. "We meet and feel good about seeing our old friends, and then go back to a life that we can have some say in the outcome. Kenny can't but he keeps on battling. I think of Kenny waking up every day and facing his challenges, and my insignificant troubles go away."

"Kenny is a very likeable guy," said Hansen. "There isn't a bad bone in his body. He never talked bad about anybody. He's a great soul with a great smile."

"There have been numerous occasions where I've been by Kenny's side hoping to lift him up and he's lifted me up," said Brookins.

Arnold continues to show the same leadership skills today as he did nearly 40 years ago during his playing days in Iowa City. His teammates recognize the significance of the example that he sets.

"Kenny's grace and strength in dealing with this situation – and his perseverance – reflects what he was like as a player," said King. "His inner strength propels him now and he inspires us."

"Life is not always a completely smooth speedway," said Gannon. "There are potholes, some big and some small. But you get yourself up and you keep moving. Kenny never complained, there is always a smile on his face. Kenny, through his faith, never asking 'Why me?' and his positive attitude, lifts all of us in times when we might feel a little down."

"The biggest thing is to never give up," said Waite. "That's Kenny. So many of us who are very fortunate, we can take something from that. Look at the bright side of things and try to have a smile on our faces. Just look at Kenny and how he represents himself."

Hogue noted a contrast between Arnold and Henry. "Kenny and Tree always struck me as opposite personalities … Kenny was always very reserved and kind of shy, while Tree was much more exuberant and effusive," he said. "Their lifelong bond is a testament to both of them. It's an extraordinary tale of love."

In Room 223 at Symphony of Morgan Park in Chicago, the light flows through the nursing home window, across the room like a diagonal cross-court pass, coming to rest at the feet of the six-foot-nine man sitting in a chair next to the bed.

Kenny Arnold lays in the bed a couple of feet away. He appears at peace as he stares out the window, the origin of the light. Mike Henry sits in the chair with his arms folded and he also gazes across the room.

But for Henry, the source of the light doesn't come from the window. It comes from Arnold.

"When you see his smile and the look in his eyes, it's like there a halo there, making everything brighter," said Henry.

That light shines from a friendship that over the course of 42 years has seen all the highs that basketball glory provides … and the lows that a battle with brain cancer delivers. It is born out of knowing that – regardless of circumstances – one person will always be there for the other. The friendship has been tested repeatedly and with each passing year, has only grown stronger.

It's an unbreakable bond and it's mutually understood.

"Every time I come here to see Kenny, I think I'm going to cheer *him* up … and every time I leave, it's actually the other way around," said Henry. "He's made *me* feel better."

Henry turns to look at Arnold, who looks back at Henry and smiles. Henry reaches out his right arm and gently taps Arnold in the left shoulder with his fist. Arnold's smile widens and he reaches out with his left arm and punches Henry in the shoulder right back.

They both laugh quietly.

Then Henry asks Arnold a question, "What do you think of what we've tried to do with the 'Teammates For Life' idea?"

Arnold looks at Henry, extends his left arm again and grabs Henry's hand, squeezing it. There are tears starting to well in Arnold's eyes and he nods.

"We know each other so well that a squeeze of the hand is all that needs to be said," said Henry.

CHAPTER 12

Time To Rest

On Thursday, April 18, 2019 at around 10 p.m., Mike Henry called me. He was on his way home from seeing Kenny Arnold at the nursing home in Chicago. In the past, when we would have these conversations, Henry would update me about how Arnold was doing and laugh about a story or two from their time together that day. But it was clear from the moment I answered the phone that night, this conversation would be different. Henry's demeanor, which was usually upbeat, was somber. It had not been a good day.

I was aware that, due to pain in Arnold's shoulder and hip, he had stopped attending physical therapy sessions a few months earlier. That made it impossible for Arnold to maintain his strength and unfortunately, his pain had intensified.

Henry explained to me that Arnold had taken a turn for the worse in the last week or so … and that his pain was excruciating again. Arnold's weight had decreased. He wasn't responding like normal to people in the room with him. Henry told me that, on this day, Arnold's eyes were rarely open and that the main goal now was for pain management. A meeting with hospice workers was scheduled to take place in a few days.

Fighting through tears, Henry said he knew that time was very short and his only wish for Arnold was to be pain-free.

After a 20-minute conversation with Henry about how dire the situation had become, I suggested to him that he tell Arnold that it would be OK for him to go, if he was ready … and to let him know that everyone else would be all right. Henry said that he thought about saying that this evening when he was with Arnold but was too emotional to get the words out.

"I'll tell him tomorrow," he said.

Before we hung up, I told Henry the world would be infinitely better if everyone had a friend like he had been for Arnold. As it turned out, these words would be spoken by dozens of people in the next few weeks.

———————————

The next several days were difficult. Henry drove to see Arnold at the nursing home daily. Arnold was conscious occasionally, but in pain almost constantly.

Henry met with the hospice team on Wednesday night, April 24, and the decision was made to provide Arnold with oxygen and morphine to help him rest without pain.

"I just wanted Kenny to be comfortable," said Henry.

That night, Henry sent out text messages to several of Arnold's friends and former teammates, letting them know the current situation and that time was short. "It was hard to say those words," said Henry. "It brought home the reality of it all."

On Thursday morning, April 25, Henry went to his job as a security guard at Valley View Early Childhood Center in Romeoville at 8:30 a.m.

"I was there for about an hour," said Henry. "But I completely fell apart in tears just thinking about Kenny. The people at work kicked me out and told me, 'Go do what you've got to do.'"

Henry drove to the nursing home. "Just that Kenny wasn't alone was important to me," he said.

Henry arrived in Arnold's room at about 10:30 a.m. John Streif drove in from Iowa City and arrived around noon. Jackie Reed came later that afternoon. They stayed with Arnold all day, trading stories with each other and hoping to provide some comfort for Arnold ... and for each other.

Arnold's brother David, and several nieces and nephews, stopped by to see Arnold at various times that day, as well.

"John and I asked the staff if we could stay the night with Kenny," said Henry. "But they kicked us out at 8:45 that night."

On Friday morning, April 26, Streif arrived at the nursing home at 6 a.m. and Henry followed at 10 a.m.

"The doctors and nurses were giving us the countdown based on Kenny's vitals," said Henry. "And in typical 'Kenny fashion,' he remained strong and kept fighting."

Henry sent me a message at 2:20 p.m. that Kenny was still battling and they were keeping him comfortable, hoping to make it a peaceful transition.

Again, just like the day before, Streif, Reed and Henry were with Kenny throughout the day, with family members stopping by, as well.

"Everybody left around 10 p.m. except me," said Henry.

Henry stayed with Arnold, sitting in a chair directly beside his bed. Henry's right hand held Arnold's left hand. Occasionally, Henry would pat Arnold's chest with his left hand, passing along words of comfort.

"I told Kenny it was OK for him to go," said Henry. "I told him, 'We'll all be OK ... and we'll all stick together. It's OK to stop fighting. It's time to rest.' It was very peaceful."

A nurse checked in on Arnold's condition every half-hour through the night. Henry stayed awake the entire time.

"At 4 a.m., a nurse checked on him and left," said Henry. "I was watching Kenny ... his breathing was normal. After a few minutes, I looked away and when I looked back, his chest wasn't moving. There was no sign of distress. He was gone."

Kenny Arnold died at 4:19 a.m. on April 27, 2019. Mike Henry was at his side.

The funeral was on Monday, May 6 at Chicago Embassy Church on South Greenwood in Chicago. There was a "Time of Remembrance" from 11 a.m. until noon, with the service after that.

I brought my son Ben (now 16 years old) with me to Chicago for the funeral. We met Henry and Brookins in Bolingbrook that morning and followed them into the city to the church.

As we drove up to the church, Ben and I each made note of the dozens of beautiful, old homes in this neighborhood. As we approached the church address, there were several signs noting that this street is a private area. It turns out that this church happens to be located directly across the street from President Obama's home in Chicago.

We arrived at 9:30 a.m. and parked in the small parking lot next to the church. Henry and Brookins parked their car in the same lot, as well. It was a beautiful spring day, with a slight breeze and temperatures in the 60s.

The four of us walked into the church and were greeted by Michael Payne and Tony Martin, who were both just inside the front door. Martin grew up in the same neighborhood as Arnold and they played basketball together back in grammar school, he said. Martin, who was a few years younger than

Arnold, eventually played college ball at the University of Wyoming and was drafted by the Golden State Warriors.

The six of us arrived 90 minutes early, just in case we were needed to help with anything. As it turned out, that was a good decision.

Shortly before 10 a.m., a woman walked up to our group in the lobby area by the front door. She said that the body had arrived and they would need help bringing it into the church.

We saw the hearse park in the street in front of the church, so the six of us – Henry, Brookins, Payne, Martin, Ben and me – walked down the sidewalk toward the vehicle. We stood behind the hearse as the driver wheeled the casket trolley close and then opened the back door. Each of us held part of the casket as we lifted it out of the hearse and placed it on the trolley. We continued to hold it as we wheeled it up to the front doors of the church.

It was a poignant moment that affected each of us. I don't recall a word being said.

"We got to the church early in case we were needed," said Henry. "We were able to carry out that last moment and bring Kenny into the church. It's something I'll always remember."

For the next couple of hours prior to the funeral service, people began filing into the church lobby. There were Arnold's family members, his classmates from Calumet High School, his friends from yesteryear and people who knew him recently.

Then there were Arnold's Hawkeye teammates and friends. One after another, they came walking in the door.

Ronnie Lester, John Streif, Coach Johnie Butler, Waymond King, Bobby Hansen, Steve Waite, Craig Anderson and Steve Krafcisin. Clay Hargrave, Jon Darsee, Rodell Davis and Mark Gannon. Todd Berkenpas arrived wearing his "Teammates For Life" shirt under his sports coat. Nannette Henry Combs, Jackie Reed, Mike Dochterman and Sara Parker. Current Hawkeye Coach Fran McCaffery and Assistant Coach Kirk Speraw made the trip from Iowa City, while former Iowa Assistant Coach Tony McAndrews made the trip from Florida. Bob Gartner wore his "Teammates For Life" shirt under his dress shirt. And on and on.

It was an impressive turnout of Hawkeyes who came to pay their respects to a man who had inspired them all.

———————————

Shortly before noon, Ben and I entered the church. There were beautiful stained-glass windows, burgundy seats and a high ceiling. The casket was in front of the church, with flowers displayed on both sides. To the far left of the flowers were two posters of Arnold during his Hawkeye playing days mounted on easels. To the far right of the flowers were two more posters of Arnold during his days as an Iowa basketball player.

We sat in the second row on the left side of the church, directly behind Henry, Butler, Payne and Brookins.

There was a keyboard player and a drummer in front of the church, behind the lectern, who played music throughout the service.

Pastor Christopher Butler delivered the eulogy. He described life as "a team sport." He talked about watching sports on TV and how the analysts always have a set of "keys to the game" that they examine to help determine what each team needs to achieve to be successful.

Pastor Butler talked about his four keys to play the game of life at a high level.

His first key was to "be a good teammate." I felt that was an outstanding place to start. Arnold had been a great team-mate on the court … and then an outstanding teammate off the court. He was surrounded by "teammates" who supported each other throughout the years as Arnold's health struggles continued. Different people played different roles throughout Arnold's life and because of his positive spirit and character, he kept everyone together.

Pastor Butler's second key was to "make in-game adjust-ments." He talked about taking on adversity and how to respond when our plans are disrupted. When Arnold was 25 years old and trying to catch on with a professional basketball team, he was diagnosed with a brain tumor. That scenario called for a dramatic shift in priorities and possibilities for a young man with such a bright future. I don't imagine anyone could've adjusted to this new reality with more grace or strength than Arnold managed to display.

The third key was to "finish strong." Arnold continued to fight with courage and toughness – while remaining positive and full of faith – right to the end. He remained an inspiration to all who knew him throughout his health struggles, but perhaps especially in the last few years as more and more people became aware of his battle and how he had persevered.

Pastor Butler's final key was to "study the greats." He said that young, hopeful basketball players study the moves and skills of someone like Michael Jordan. It makes sense that if we want to be successful in the game of life, we need to take a good look at the people who we think have been successful in that arena and emulate them, as well. He discussed how much we all respect how Arnold had lived his life, handled adversity and remained a positive role model for so many people. Pastor Butler suggested that we continue to talk about Arnold's example, reflect on it and see if we could incorporate some of those character traits into our own lives.

Several people spoke during the funeral service. We were told how Arnold's nickname as a youngster was "Froggy." We learned how Arnold had directed one of his nephews to find his passion and choose his path accordingly. We heard numerous stories about Arnold's humility, toughness, competitive nature and ever-present smile. Coach Butler called him a "winner" who "ran his race to the very last day."

Another speaker asked Henry to stand up and while fighting through tears, he said of Henry, "He's my hero." The entire congregation stood and applauded.

An old friend of Arnold's mentioned the saying, "some birds aren't meant to be caged." Then he asked the people from Kenny's "Hawkeye Family" to stand and he said, "We let Kenny go ... and the people of Iowa took care of him. We appreciate you." The rest of the congregation applauded again.

Mike "Tree" Henry stood behind the lectern to share his comments about Arnold. Somehow, he maintained his composure and his voice didn't crack. He reminded everyone that he and Arnold were born on the same day, June 7, 1959 ... and they had been best friends from the first day they met.

"Throughout all the years that Kenny struggled with his illness, he never complained," said Henry. "Kenny never asked, 'Why me?' And he was grateful for everything that people did for him."

Then he shared a story from several years ago that described how Arnold's strong faith helped him get through all the adversity he faced.

"Vince (Brookins) had driven into Chicago from Cleveland to see Kenny at the nursing home," said Henry. "The three of us were talking, catching up. Vince and I figured we were going to cheer Kenny up that day.

"Kenny asked how we were doing. Vince and I each shared some stuff that we were going through, some challenges we were facing. And when we were done talking, Kenny looked at us and asked, 'Can I pray for you?'

"So there we were, the three of us, standing and holding hands in a circle as Kenny led us in a prayer, asking for strength and guidance. We got done with the prayer and Kenny had a smile on his face.

"Vince asked him, 'How do you do this and stay so strong? I don't think I could handle this like you.

"And Kenny answered, 'No, you couldn't. God gave me this challenge because he knew I could handle it. This is God's plan for me. I'm taking on this burden, so you don't have to suffer. I'll do that for you."

During Arnold's final days at the nursing home, one former Hawkeye teammate wrote a letter to Arnold. It was important to him to share his thoughts with Arnold while he was still able to hear them, so he called Henry on the phone and asked if he could read the letter to Arnold. Henry put his cell phone on "speaker" and held the phone up to Arnold's ear.

Here is the text of that letter:

"Kenny, I want to make sure you get the love and recognition you deserve. And a proper 'thank you' for being in our lives.

"Thank you:

"For being an integral part of my life from my formative college years through and into adulthood.

"For being a true example of what Grace and Courage are during the most difficult of life circumstances.

"For reminding all of us that what's truly most important has nothing to do with material things.

"For creating a living legacy in ALL of us – for the rest of our lives.

"For always being our 'point guard,' the floor leader. Leading us, showing the way and keeping our team together.

"For being a hero to millions of people with your strength and humility.

"For loving us unconditionally in your special way.

"You've fought a hard, difficult battle with a will most of us can only hope to have. You've challenged us to look in the mirror and see who and what we really are. You've brought out the best and most sensitive sides of us. You've helped us keep this life 'thing' in perspective. You've left an impression on me, and everyone you've touched, to do the very best and be the very best people we can be.

"You can rest now. Job well done.

"Your spirit will live eternally in all of us.

"I love you, my friend."

Henry held Arnold's hand while the letter was read to him. Arnold nodded his head as he listened ... and a couple of tears formed in his eyes.

The letter is a powerful message that shines a light on Arnold's strengths and how he faced adversity. It is also an outstanding reminder to reflect on his spirit, courage and grace as we face our own struggles along the way.

"It was so great that Kenny got to hear that," said Henry. "It really expressed what all of us felt, but just couldn't say."

It was one more thank you – and good-bye – from Arnold's teammates. His teammates for life.

EPILOGUE

Inspired by the events of the last four decades, the Kenny Arnold Foundation has been established to raise funds for cancer research and related charities. A website has been created at KennyArnoldFoundation.org that provides current information, including photos, videos and links to stories from various media outlets.

Arnold's "Teammates For Life" host an annual golf outing each summer at Buena Vista University Golf Course at Lake Creek Country Club in Storm Lake, Iowa. There are other events and fundraisers being planned, as well. New information about upcoming events is posted on the foundation's website and on Kenny Arnold's Facebook page.

——————————

On April 4, 2018, Mike Arens, a member of Iowa's Final Four team in 1980, passed away suddenly at the age of 60. I had the pleasure of getting to know Mike as he was at the nursing home in Chicago the day Matt Dunning and I arrived to help Kenny Arnold try a speech-generating device. Then I saw Mike at a couple of events in the following year or so … he was always engaging and smiling.

I didn't know Mike well, but from my limited time around him, I know a couple of things. First, he was enormously proud to be a part of the Hawkeye Basketball Family and the 1980 Final Four team. When the stories about that team and those games started flying around, Mike's smile widened and his laughter grew. I knew Mike as a fun-loving person, who was gregarious and had a self-deprecating sense of humor. He fit right in with the "Teammates For Life" who have stuck together all these years.

And second, I know that he is missed.

I am so grateful that my family has been able to witness so much of this story up close and in person. My son Ben, for example, will always have wonderful memories of seeing people treat each other with kindness and compassion in challenging situations that otherwise, he may never have witnessed.

I am thankful to have gotten to know people like Kenny Arnold, Mike Henry, Vince Brookins, Ronnie Lester, Bobby Hansen, Johnie Butler, Jackie Reed, Steve Waite, John Streif, Michael Payne, Nannette Henry Combs, Waymond King, Mark Gannon, Kevin Boyle, Steve Carfino and all the rest of the Hawkeye Basketball Family.

I believe this is a wonderful story about how Coach Lute Olson assembled a college basketball team by selectively recruiting young men who were unselfish, determined, positive and shared a willingness to do whatever it takes … and as these men grew older and tackled life's greatest challenges, they continued to display the character that had earned them so much success on the basketball court decades earlier.

I will miss Kenny ... and getting Tree's updates on how he's doing.

But I will try to always remember the example that Kenny, Tree and their "Teammates For Life" have shown as I face any future challenges in my life, and as I provide support for those I love.

Thanks for reading.